IMMIGRATION

Everyday Life:

WALTER A. HAZEN

Good Year Books

An Imprint of Pearson Learning

Photo Credits
Unless otherwise acknowledged, all photographs are the property of Scott Foresman and Company. Page abbreviations are as follows: (T)top, (C)center, (B)bottom, (L)left, (R)right. Cover(L) UPI/Corbis-Bettmann. (R)Corbis-Bettmann (Background) AP/Wide World. 2 The Granger Collection. 3 Corbis-Bettmann. 4(T) Corbis-Bettmann. (B) The Granger Collection. 5 The Granger Collection. 10 The Granger Collection. 11(T) The Granger Collection. (B)Library of Congress. 12 The Granger Collection. 18 The Granger Collection. 19 Corbis-Bettmann. 20 Corbis-Bettmann. 21 New York Public Library, Astor Lenox, Tilden Foundation. 26 Corbis. 27 Library of Congress. 28 The Granger Collection. 29 The Granger Collection. 34 Corbis-Bettmann. 35 Library of Congress. 36 The Granger Collection. 37 The Granger Collection. 42 The Granger Collection. 43 UPI/Corbis-Bettmann. 44 Library of Congress. 45(T) Corbis/Baldwin H. Ward (B)UPI/Corbis-Bettmann. 50 Corbis-Bettmann. 51 The Granger Collection. 52 The Granger Collection. 53 Corbis-Bettmann. 58 The Granger Collection. 59 The Granger Collection. 60 Corbis-Bettmann. 61 Corbis-Bettmann. 66 Corbis-Bettmann. 67 UPI/Corbis-Bettmann. 68 UPI/Corbis-Bettmann. 69(T) Library of Congress (B) The Granger Collection. 74 Corbis/Reuters. 75 H. Armstrong Roberts. 76 Corbis. 77(T) Corbis-Bettmann (B) Corbis/Bettmann-UPI. 82 Corbis/Bettmann-UPI. 83 Agence France Presse/Corbis-Bettmann. 84 Corbis-Bettmann. 85 Corbis/Bettmann-UPI.

Dedication
To Martha, Jordan, and Allison

Acknowledgments
Grateful acknowledgment to my editor, Laura Strom, who has guided me through several books in Good Year's "Everyday Life" series. Without her advice and support, this book would not have been possible.

I would also like to thank Roberta Dempsey, Acquisitions Manager at Good Year, for giving me the opportunity to be a part of such an exciting project. Her support and confidence in me is likewise appreciated.

Good Year Books

are available for most basic curriculum subjects plus many enrichment areas. For more Good Year Books, contact your local bookseller or educational dealer. For a complete catalog with information about other Good Year Books, please write to:

Good Year Books
An imprint of Pearson Learning
299 Jefferson Road
Parsippany, New Jersey 07054-0480
1-800-321-3106
www.pearsonlearning.com

Design and Illustration: Sean O'Neill, Ronan Design

Editor: Laura Layton Strom

Editorial Manager: Suzanne Beason

Executive Editor: Judy Adams

Publisher: Rosemary Calicchio

Table of Contents

From Everyday Life: Immigration ©Good Year Books.

Table of Contents *continued*

Introduction

The story of immigration began during colonial times and continues today. It is the story of men, women, and children who risked and are continuing to risk everything to achieve the American Dream. Some have succeeded; many have not.

The story of immigration is really two stories. The first took place in the years before the Civil War, when the United States was still a young nation. During this time, workers were needed to build the roads, bridges, canals, railroads, and cities that made America what it is today. Immigrants who came primarily from northern and western Europe filled this need. Most—except for the Irish, who were discriminated against because of their religion—were welcome.

Attitudes toward immigration began to change drastically after 1880. Two factors brought about this change. First, jobs and land were no longer plentiful and so Americans found themselves in stiff competition with immigrants, whose numbers increased each year. Second, immigrants who came after 1880 were mostly from southern and eastern Europe. Most were poor, unskilled peasants and laborers who were misunderstood and resented by many Americans. They dressed differently, spoke different languages, and had different customs and religious beliefs. Because of these differences, they experienced more prejudice and discrimination than those who came before them.

In *Everyday Life: Immigration*, you will learn about immigrants who came during both these periods. You will share their hopes and disappointments and their successes and failures. Theirs is a story that is not altogether a happy one, but it is one you should find interesting.

Walter A. Hazen

CHAPTER I

Coming as Colonists: Why They Came

The first immigrants to arrive in America were people textbooks refer to as colonists. The majority came from England, but there were also a large number from France and Holland. Others came from Sweden, Finland, Ireland, Scotland, Spain, and what would in time become Germany. They represented every walk of life and practiced every religious faith. They included Protestants, Catholics, Jews, and even people who professed no religious beliefs at all. A few were well off, but most were poor or mistreated folk who had left their homelands in search of a better life in a new country.

Although the French and the Spanish were the first to establish settlements in America, it was primarily the English who colonized the region that in time became the thirteen colonies. The English settled along the Atlantic coast in a narrow stretch of land extending from Maine southward to where Spanish Florida began. At first, while land was plentiful, they were content to stay where they were. In fact, British law forbade settling beyond the Appalachian Mountains for fear of stirring up the Native Americans who lived there. But when all available land along the coast was taken, some settlers ignored the British king's law and started to push westward.

The English first attempted to establish a colony on Roanoke Island off the coast of North Carolina. They tried several times in the 1580s, and each attempt failed. The last group to occupy the small settlement disappeared without a trace around 1587. Because the word "Croatoan" was found carved on a tree at the site, some historians believe the settlers may have been taken away by an Indian tribe of that name.

The first permanent English settlement was established at Jamestown, Virginia, in 1607. It was founded by some 100 men, over half of whom were gentlemen, or landed gentry. Landed gentry were wealthy English landowners who belonged to a class just below the nobility. They came not for land or religious freedom but to search for gold. They brought only the clothes on their backs and would have starved to death were it not for the leadership of an able leader named John Smith. Although they found no gold or other riches, these early settlers eventually turned Virginia into a thriving colony based on the growing of tobacco.

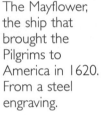

The Mayflower, the ship that brought the Pilgrims to America in 1620. From a steel engraving.

From *Everyday Life: Immigration* © Good Year Books.

Thirteen years after Jamestown was founded, a second English colony sprang up at Plymouth in Massachusetts. It was started by the Pilgrims, or Separatists. The Pilgrims were part of a group known as Puritans who wanted to "purify," or make more simple, the teachings and practices of the Church of England. But the Pilgrims went farther than most Puritans in that they chose to separate themselves completely from the established church and worship as they pleased. For this reason they were persecuted and had to leave the country. That is how they came to be called Pilgrims, which means people who take long journeys for religious reasons.

At first the Pilgrims went to Holland. Holland was a tolerant nation that permitted people of every religious belief to live there. The Pilgrims stayed in Holland for twelve years, where they prospered and were well treated by the Dutch people. But they were not happy. Their children started imitating Dutch ways and dress and going to Dutch churches. Many of their sons when they grew up either joined the Dutch army or sailed away on Dutch ships. Elder Pilgrims began to worry that their group would lose its identity and their children would become more Dutch than English. For this reason the Pilgrims set sail for America and the Atlantic coast in 1620.

Braving rough waters, a group of Puritans makes its way to a waiting ship that will take them to America. From an undated engraving.

Sailing the Atlantic Ocean in the 1600s was a dangerous undertaking. Although all except two of the 102 passengers aboard the *Mayflower* (the Pilgrim's ship) survived the long voyage, many of those who came on later voyages were not so lucky. Elderly passengers and young children often died during the crossing. One man who kept a diary aboard his ship recorded that thirty-two children died at sea and that their bodies were thrown overboard by their grieving parents. Many of those who lived through such terrible journeys suffered from seasickness, boils, scurvy, dysentery, lice, and other miseries. And, if these ailments were not enough, they had to eat biscuits that were full of worms and spiders' nests!

In spite of the hardships of an Atlantic crossing, people continued to come by the thousands. In 1628 Puritans founded the colony of Massachusetts Bay on the site where Salem now stands. They too were dissatisfied with the Church of England and came to America to worship as they saw fit. King Charles I seemed more than happy to grant them a charter

To the jeers of English spectators, a Quaker is flogged. Quakers who settled among the Puritans in Massachusetts often met the same fate.

Pilgrims on their way to church in Plymouth. Note their guns, which they carried in the event of an Indian attack. From a painting by George Henry Boughton.

for land north of Plymouth, since many in their group were well-to-do gentry who were beginning to cause problems for the Crown.

About 400 men, women, and children crossed the Atlantic and established the Massachusetts Bay Colony. More ships came later, and within a few years the colony numbered more than 4,000 people. Unlike the settlers at Jamestown and Plymouth, the Puritans came well supplied and were better able to survive the hardships of those early years. They experienced no "starving time" during their first winter in the New World.

Although the Puritans came to America seeking religious freedom, they were not willing to grant this freedom to others who settled among them. Non-Puritan residents could not hold office and were required to pay taxes to support the Congregational Church, as the church of the Puritans came to be called. Some settlers, such as the peaceful Quakers, were flogged and even hanged.

Intolerance on the part of the Massachusetts Bay Colony caused some members to be either banished or compelled to leave on their own. The colonies of Rhode Island and Connecticut were founded in this manner. Roger Williams was a Puritan who believed that all people should be allowed to worship as they pleased. He was forced to leave Massachusetts and, as a result, went on to found the colony of Rhode Island. Thomas Hooker was a minister who thought everybody should be allowed to vote, whether they belonged to the Congregational Church or not. He too left Massachusetts Bay and founded the colony of Connecticut.

In time, settlers from England established other colonies along the Atlantic Coast. But there were also immigrants who came from other countries and started settlements of their own. Not the least of these were the Dutch, who settled in the area that later became New York. They called their colony New Amsterdam, after the name of their capital city in The Netherlands. (The Netherlands, which means "low countries," was sometimes called Holland. But to be accurate, Holland was the name that applied to only two of the provinces, or sections, of that country.)

The Dutch who migrated to the lower Hudson River area of New York came because of fertile land and the possibility of a rich fur trade. They founded New Amsterdam in 1623 and

From *Everyday Life: Immigration* ©Good Year Books.

controlled it until 1664, when it was seized by the English. The English changed the name of New Amsterdam to New York City, and that of New Netherlands, which the expanded Dutch colony was called, to New York.

The Quakers were another group to establish a settlement in the 1600s. Led by William Penn, the Quakers not only believed in religious freedom but complete equality as well. They founded Pennsylvania, meaning "Penn's Woods," in 1681. Because of liberal practices and fair treatment of the Indians, which resulted in few attacks on colonists, Pennsylvania grew quickly in population.

William Penn signs his first treaty with the Native Americans in 1682. Penn and the Quakers established friendly relations with the Indians of Pennsylvania.

To this point you have learned that people came to America for a variety of reasons. Some came seeking gold or other riches. Many came for religious freedom or for the promise of fertile farmland. Still others came to escape political persecution. The latter was especially true of people of the Jewish faith, who were often the victims of planned pogroms (massacres) in their home countries.

During pogroms, police and soldiers often stood by while mobs attacked and killed whole communities of Jews. Sometimes the police and soldiers participated in the killings themselves. Pogroms had occurred in Europe for centuries and became particularly severe in the 1800s.

Not a few settlers came to America to escape spending their lives in prison. In England at the time, jails were full of people imprisoned for stealing food or being unable to pay off small debts. With no hope of ever being released, many accepted the English government's offer of freedom in exchange for sailing to America. Georgia was founded in this way as a "debtor's colony" by James Oglethorpe in 1732. Even after the colonies were well established, thousands of prisoners—some of them hardened criminals—continued to be sent to America.

The list of immigrants to America in the 1600s and 1700s goes on. Swedes settled in what later became Delaware and, before the area fell under Dutch rule, made a lasting contribution to the American frontier: the log cabin. There were also Finns, Scots, and Irish who came looking for a better way of life. Finally, there were the French, who came primarily because of the fur trade. They settled in the area of the Great Lakes, the Mississippi and Ohio Valleys, and Canada.

From Everyday Life: Immigration © Good Year Books.

Name _____ Date _____

Draw a Picture

Draw and color a picture of the *Mayflower*, the ship that brought the Pilgrims to America in 1620. You can find a picture of the *Mayflower* on page 2 and in most textbooks and encyclopedias, or in a book dealing with the founding of the English colonies.

From *Everyday Life: Immigration* ©Good Year Books.

Name _____ Date _____

Create a Dialogue

Jonathan and Sarah Carver have a difficult decision to make. They have heard that Thomas Hooker and others are planning to leave the Massachusetts Bay Colony to establish a new settlement somewhere in the Connecticut Valley to the west. Because they, like Hooker, believe that all people are equal and have the right to govern themselves, they would very much like to go.

On the other hand, the Carvers are concerned about Mary and James, their young children. Will they be safe in the wilderness? Will the Indians who live in the Connecticut Valley prove friendly or hostile? Should the family leave secure Salem and embark on an adventure full of uncertainties?

On the lines provided, create a dialogue between the Carvers in which they weigh the pros and cons of accompanying Hooker and his party.

_____

_____

_____

_____

_____

_____

_____

_____

_____

_____

_____

_____

_____

_____

_____

_____

_____

_____

Name _____ Date _____

Distinguish Between Fact and Opinion

Can you tell the difference between a fact and an opinion? Sometimes it is not easy to do. Every day we make statements we think are facts but which are really opinions. Facts are things that are true and can be proven; opinions are simply strong beliefs.

Carefully read the sentences. Then on the blank line to the left of each, write **F** if you think the statement is a fact. Write **O** if you think it is only an opinion.

_____ 1. Most of the colonists who settled along the Atlantic Coast of America came from England.

_____ 2. The French and the Spanish were the first to establish settlements in North America.

_____ 3. The settlers of the early colony at Roanoke Island were probably all killed by Native Americans.

_____ 4. Jamestown was the first permanent English settlement in America.

_____ 5. The Pilgrims, who lived in Holland for twelve years, considered the Dutch way of life inferior to that of their own.

_____ 6. The Puritans were more intolerant of opposing religious beliefs than the Church of England from which they had fled.

_____ 7. All Puritans favored severe punishment for Quakers and others who held opinions different from their own.

_____ 8. Unlike the Pilgrims, the Puritans did not favor breaking away from the Church of England.

_____ 9. Convicts released from English jails made poor colonists when they came to America.

_____ 10. Georgia was founded as a debtor's colony.

_____ 11. The Quakers offered equality and religious freedom to any settler who came to Pennsylvania.

_____ 12. All colonists considered Indians savages and thought they should be eliminated.

_____ 13. The Swedes are generally given credit for introducing the log cabin to America.

From Everyday Life: Immigration ©Good Year Books.

Name _____ Date _____

Find the Main Idea

Most paragraphs contain one central, or main, idea. How good are you at picking these out?

Refer to the Chapter 1 narrative text you just read. On the lines following the paragraph numbers at right, write what you consider to be the main idea expressed in each paragraph.

Paragraph 1

_____

_____

_____

Paragraph 6

_____

_____

_____

Paragraph 7

_____

_____

_____

Paragraph 10

_____

_____

_____

Paragraph 14

_____

_____

_____

Paragraph 17

_____

_____

_____

Being Forced to Come

You learned in Chapter 1 that many people did not come to America of their own free will. The King of England sometimes emptied his jails by sending what he considered undesirable elements to the New World. You should remember that thousands of these ex-convicts were not merely poor people who had fallen into debt and ended up in prison. Their numbers included such hardened criminals as rapists and murderers.

Be that as it may, by far the largest number of unwilling immigrants to America were African slaves. Estimates vary, but some historians place the number of Africans forced into slavery in the New World at between 10 and 20 million. Most of these became the slaves of the Portuguese in Brazil and the Spaniards in Mexico, Peru, and the West Indies. The others, numbering somewhere between 400,000 and 1,200,000, became slaves in the English colonies in North America. Of this group the large majority were sent to the South, where a combination of favorable climate and fertile soil made large plantations possible.

It may surprise you to learn that the first Africans to set foot in the New World did not come as slaves. They came as free men. Blacks were members of the expeditions of Columbus, Balboa, Cortés, and Pizarro. One black, named Estevanico, even led an expedition of his own. He explored and helped open up what is now Arizona and New Mexico for Spain.

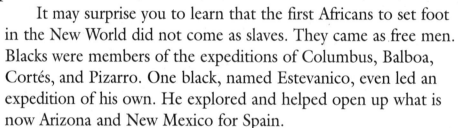

Estevanico, a free black who led an expedition into the Southwest in search of the mythical Seven (golden) Cities of Cibola.

How did the African slave trade come about? In 1441 a Portuguese sea captain named Gonsalves captured twelve blacks off the west coast of Africa. He took them home to Portugal and sold them as slaves. As the years passed, more and more Africans were captured or bought from various African tribes and taken to Portugal. Soon the Portuguese had so many slaves that they began selling some of them to the Spanish. In both countries African slaves were often given their freedom, after which they were granted the same rights as ordinary citizens. That is how some of them came to accompany Spanish explorers to the New World.

At first only the Portuguese and the Spanish were involved in the African slave trade. Then, in the early 1600s, England and other nations joined in. The first Africans to be brought to North America arrived in a Dutch ship at Jamestown, Virginia, on August 20, 1619. They numbered twenty, and they

were sold as indentured servants rather than as true slaves. All eventually won their freedom. Several became large landholders and came to own slaves themselves.

The status of Africans in Virginia and elsewhere changed after a few years. In 1661 the Virginia colonial legislature passed a law that made permanent slaves of black workers and their children. Maryland passed a similar law, and most of the other colonies followed suit. In just a few short years, the fate of Africans in America was sealed. Virginia even passed a law in 1669 that said an owner could not be accused of murdering a slave because no master would purposely destroy his own property! Such laws opened the way for slave owners to treat their slaves any way they pleased—even kill them.

If many slaves were terribly mistreated by their colonial masters, it could be argued that their suffering was nothing compared to what they endured before their arrival. Blacks were rounded up and kept in "factories" or forts on the coast of West Africa, where they were bought, branded, and crammed into the hold of slave ships. The terrible ordeal of their crossing the Atlantic has been described by many who survived, including Olaudah Equiano.

Cramped quarters of a Spanish slave ship of the 1840s. Many slaves did not survive the terrible ordeal of an Atlantic crossing.

Olaudah Equiano was an eleven-year-old boy when he was captured by another tribe and sold to slave traders. He later said that his biggest fear was that he would be eaten by "those white men with horrible looks, red faces, and long hair." That, of course, did not happen, but what he experienced while chained to others in the bottom of a ship might have been equally as horrible.

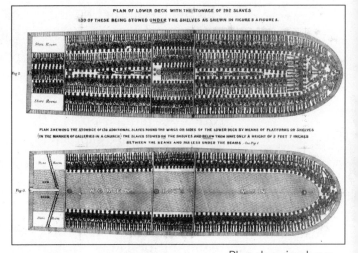

Olaudah, as did others, wrote a book relating what he went through following his capture and sale to slave traders. His description of the way in which slaves were packed into the holds of ships causes one to wonder how any of them survived. The hold, which is the area below the deck, was divided into tiers, or floors. Each tier was sometimes no higher than eighteen inches. Think about that. Eighteen inches is a foot and a half. This

Plan showing how every available space of a slave ship was utilized in carrying its human cargo. Slaves were confined to tiers ranging in height from 18 inches to about 2½ feet.

meant that slaves on some ships could neither sit or stand. They crossed the Atlantic in a prone position, chained together by twos. If a slave died on the way, he was unshackled from his partner and his body was thrown overboard.

More than a few slaves went mad during the voyage to America, which sometimes took as long as fourteen weeks. It was not uncommon for a slave to strangle the person to whom he was chained to acquire more space. The stench and heat of the confined area also took its toll on the unwilling passengers. Sometimes half the human cargo died before the ship reached the New World. But it mattered little to the slave traders. Their profits were more than high enough to offset the loss of the slaves who died.

Mutineers led by the slave Cinque seize control of the Spanish slave ship *Amistad* in June, 1839.

Not all Africans came passively to America. Some, before being pushed into the holds of ships, committed mass suicide by jumping overboard while chained together. Others mutinied and killed the crews of the slave ships. You may have seen the movie *Amistad*. The *Amistad* was a Spanish slave ship that, in 1839, fell victim to a mutiny by fifty-three slaves being transported from Havana to another port in Cuba. Led by an African named Cinque, the slaves killed the captain and crew of the ship and sailed north. (They spared one crew member to serve as navigator.) They were captured by a U.S. warship off Long Island and brought to trial. In a surprise verdict they were freed and permitted to return to Africa. It is ironic, however, that Cinque, once back in Africa, set himself up as a slave trader!

Perhaps the most famous slave rebellion was led by a Virginia slave named Nat Turner. Turner was a devoutly religious man who believed he had been chosen to lead his people out of slavery. In August, 1831, he and sixty followers went on a rampage in Southhampton County, Virginia. They killed fifty-seven whites before soldiers put down their rebellion. During the manhunt for Turner that followed, as many as one hundred innocent blacks may have been killed. Turner himself was captured and hanged along with twenty other slaves who participated in the uprising.

From *Everyday Life: Immigration* © Good Year Books.

Southern slave owners reacted to the Turner Insurrection (rebellion) by strengthening the already strict Black Codes. These codes, or laws, were intended to keep slaves "in their place" and to prevent similar uprisings from breaking out. Slaves in towns and cities were required to stay indoors at night, and those on farms and plantations could not gather in groups larger than from three to ten. Blacks could not own weapons, horses, or even boats. They could not buy or sell merchandise or enter into any kind of agreement without the permission of their owner. Further, they could not leave one plantation to visit another without written permission, and, if permission were granted, they could only stay for one hour. Any slave who violated the Black Codes might be whipped, branded, or even maimed by having a finger, hand, or ear cut off.

Some laws in the Black Codes bordered on the ridiculous. Slaves could not, for example, beat drums or blow horns for fear that such noises might be signals for an uprising. And, since legal marriages between slaves were disallowed, what sometimes passed as marriage ceremonies were equally as silly. On some plantations slaves were considered married simply by jumping together over a broomstick (under the strict supervision of the master, of course!).

In spite of such restrictive and punitive (punishing) measures as the Black Codes, the treatment of slaves in the American colonies varied from place to place and from plantation to plantation. On some large plantations, slaves had neither the time nor the energy to think of rebellion. Their workday began well before sunrise and continued until well after dark. If they slept late and did not report to the fields at the prescribed hour, they might be severely flogged and salt water poured over their raw wounds. When their workday finally ended, they ate a quick supper and collapsed in bed.

Slaves on other plantations fared better. Some had kindhearted masters who treated them well and looked after their needs. Such relationships help explain the failure of some slave rebellions, such as the one led by Denmark Vesey in 1822. That rebellion collapsed largely because one of the conspirators could not bring himself to kill his master, who had treated him kindly.

Whether treated well or brutally, the number of slaves in America increased to almost four million by the outbreak of the Civil War. Nearly all of these were located in the South. Of the eight states that had originally made up the New England and Middle Colonies, all had abolished slavery by the end of the 1700s.

Name _____ Date _____

Draw Conclusions from Your Reading

An important skill associated with reading is being able to draw conclusions. A conclusion is a judgment or opinion reached after considering the facts and information presented in a certain passage.

Read each of the following situations and draw your own conclusions to answer the questions.

1. The Southern colonies were blessed with fertile soil, a moderate climate, and a long growing season. The New England colonies, by contrast, had to endure rocky soil, harsh winters, and a short growing season.

   What role do you think climate and geography played in the strength and duration of slavery in the two regions?

   _____

   _____

   _____

2. The Spanish and the Portuguese, and to a certain extent the English, tried unsuccessfully to make slaves of the Indians and use them as laborers in mines and on plantations, but they either died in droves or repeatedly tried to run away.

   Such was not the case with slaves imported from Africa. Why do you think this was so?

   _____

   _____

   _____

3. You will remember that many slaves killed themselves before they could be locked into the holds of slave ships and sent to the New World. What conclusion can be drawn from the fact that they often jumped overboard chained together, resulting in their instant drowning?

   _____

   _____

   _____

From *Everyday Life: Immigration* © Good Year Books.

Name _____ Date _____

Interpret a Population Line Graph

You know that a line graph is a graph with a line that shows change over a period of time. The line graph at the right shows how the number of slaves in America increased rapidly between the years 1750 and 1860. Five representative years are shown, along with the approximate number of slaves for each year.

Use the information from the graph to answer the following questions.

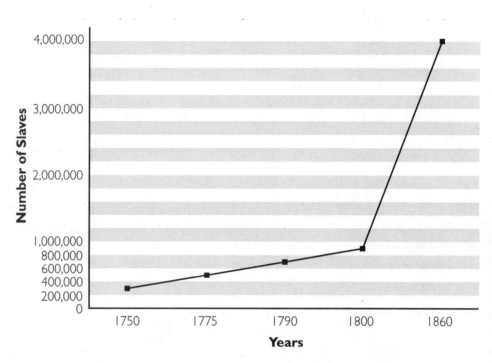

Increase in the Slave Population

Number of Slaves

Years

1. By what percent did the slave population increase between 1775 and 1860?
   _____%

2. How many more slaves were there in 1860 than in 1750?
   _____ more

3. By how many times did the slave population increase between 1750 and 1800?
   _____ times

4. How many slaves were there in 1790? _____

5. How many more slaves were there in 1800 than in 1775?
   _____ more

Name _____ Date _____

Write Your Opinion

Federal fugitive slave laws once permitted slave owners or their agents to go into any state to bring back runaway slaves. The laws further stated that local officials were expected to assist in the capture of such fugitives (runaways) and see that they were returned to their rightful owners. Any person who tried to help or hide a runaway slave could be fined or even imprisoned. Estimates place the number of runaway slaves who received assistance through the Underground Railroad at 75,000.

With the fugitive slave laws in mind, write your opinions regarding the questions at the right.

1. If you had lived in the North in the years before the Civil War, would you have become a participant in the Underground Railroad? Why or why not?

_____

_____

_____

_____

_____

2. Why do you think the United States Congress would pass legislation such as a fugitive slave law?

_____

_____

_____

_____

_____

3. Were Northerners justified in violating the fugitive slave law? Why or why not? Would you do the same with any law you considered unfair or unjust? Why or why not? Continue your answer on a separate piece of paper if necessary.

_____

_____

_____

_____

_____

From Everyday Life: Immigration ©Good Year Books.

Name _____ Date _____

Recall Information from the Narrative

The ability to recall information is a valuable skill, one that becomes even more important as you advance from one grade level to the next.

At the right are nine questions having to do with the chapter you have just read. See how many you can answer without referring back to the narrative.

1. Which country started the European slave trade in the 1400s?
   _____

2. Explain how blacks came to be part of the New World expeditions of some Spanish explorers.
   _____
   _____

3. On which coast of Africa did European nations build forts or "factories" in which they held slaves until they were bought and shipped to the New World? _____

4. Why did so many African captives die aboard slave ships before ever reaching America?
   _____
   _____
   _____

5. To which English colony were the first African slaves brought in 1619? _____

6. Who was Olaudah Equiano?
   _____
   _____

7. Describe what happened aboard the *Amistad*, as well as the final outcome of the incident.
   _____
   _____

8. For what are both Denmark Vesey and Nat Turner remembered? _____

9. What were Black Codes, and why were they enacted?
   _____
   _____

From Everyday Life: Immigration ©Good Year Books.

CHAPTER 3

Coming in the Second Wave

The first wave of immigration to America extended from the beginning of colonial times until the middle of the 1800s. During that long period, about 1.6 million people of all nationalities came to our shores. This was an average of some 7,000 immigrants a year.

By contrast, more than 1.8 million newcomers arrived from England and Ireland alone in just the ten years from 1846 to 1855. Others came mainly from Germany and the Scandinavian countries. Their migration was part of a period often referred to as the "Old Immigration," which took place between the years 1820 and 1880.

During the Old Immigration, about 7.5 million people came to America. Most were from western Europe, although there was a sprinkling of immigrants from eastern Europe and Asia. The largest of the latter group was from China. About 230,000 Chinese came to America during the period of the Old Immigration. Most helped lay track for the western part of the transcontinental railroad. In Chapter 7, you will learn of the hostility they encountered in their new environment.

Why did such a large number of immigrants come to America after 1820, and particularly after 1845? The reasons are many and varied. Most of the Irish came for the simple reason that they were starving. Many Germans emigrated to escape political persecution after the failure of several democratic revolutions. In England, the Industrial Revolution and its machines had put skilled craftsmen out of work, causing thousands of them to book passage for the New World. Further, some European cities just found it cheaper to ship their paupers out than to keep them in jails or poorhouses. Most immigrants, however, came to America hoping for a better life. Anything, they reasoned, would be preferable to what they were leaving behind in Europe.

The case of the Irish was a particularly sad one. A disastrous potato blight (plant disease) in 1845 wiped out this staple crop and resulted in almost a million peasants starving to death. Ireland's poor were reduced to stealing or eating grass just to stay alive. It was

A wood engraving of a peasant's hut graphically depicts the hunger caused by the Irish potato crop failure of 1845. Almost a million Irish peasants starved to death in one year.

From *Everyday Life: Immigration* © Good Year Books.

a common sight to see people dying in the streets with green froth from eating grass oozing from their mouths.

Not all immigrants came to America because they were starving or had been persecuted for their political or religious beliefs. As previously mentioned, many came hoping to improve their quality of life. They were lured by attractive wall posters and newspaper advertisements paid for by railroad companies and steamship lines. America was pictured as a land of immense opportunity— a land where all people were equal and those willing to work hard would succeed beyond their wildest dreams. Some states went so far as to promise immigrants the right to vote even before they became citizens.

In an illustration from the late 1800s, starving and homeless Irish families on the left contrast sharply with Queen Victoria's Jubilee celebration on the right.

Other immigrants were persuaded to come because of letters they received from relatives and friends who had emigrated earlier. Many of these letters, of course, stretched the truth a bit. Some told how even the poorest families ate three sumptuous meals a day, their tables always filled with good bread and various kinds of meat. "Come to America; you will be happy and independent here" was the theme that ran through such letters. Had you lived at the time and been already settled in America, would you have told friends and family any differently?

Regardless of why they came, most immigrants certainly did not find that "getting here was half the fun," as the saying goes. Quite the contrary was true. Both the trip to the port where they boarded their ship and the voyage across the ocean were trying experiences. Many lost everything they had before ever sailing, while countless others did not survive the Atlantic crossing. (The story of the emigrants' ordeal at sea is covered in Chapter 4.)

Many people tried to take advantage of poor emigrants. If the emigrants were not robbed en route to their port city, they were likely to be plundered upon arrival. Some of the worst offenders were porters called runners. In Liverpool, where most emigrants shipped out, there was a particularly dishonest group of tough runners known as the Forty Thieves. They charged outrageous prices to carry luggage, heavy trunks, and boxes, and were not above forcing their services upon hapless emigrants. If an emigrant refused to turn his or her belongings over to a runner, the runner might snatch the luggage away and refuse to give it back until he had received his fee.

Runners often worked hand in hand with merchants and boardinghouse keepers who paid them a percentage for guiding unsuspecting emigrants their way. Emigrants were literally dragged into shops, where they were tricked into buying bad food and supplies for which they had no use at all. Instead of being led to respectable lodging places, they were directed to dilapidated boardinghouses. The keepers then took their money and crammed them into cellars; it was not unusual for thirty emigrants to be boarded in a cellar at one time.

If newly arrived immigrants thought things would be better in New York, the usual port of entry, they were in for a surprise. New York City had just as many dishonest runners as Liverpool. There were also swindlers who sold naive immigrants everything from fake railroad tickets to deeds for land that turned out to be underwater. So many people cheated the immigrants that a Swedish minister remarked that Americans rivaled mosquitoes in the way they bled foreigners dry.

In spite of being cheated at every turn and facing discrimination and sometimes violent hostility, most immigrants saw America as the land of promise. Many of them had left homelands where political freedom was only a dream and where empty plates and starving people were commonplace. In America jobs were plentiful and land was cheap. Some immigrants who came over in the Old Immigration returned to their native lands, but most stayed.

A political cartoon by Thomas Nast shows the "Herald of Relief" imploring America to send aid to Ireland's starving peasants.

Where did immigrants go after landing at New York and other ports of entry? Most stayed in the northeast and found jobs in the ever growing factories or elsewhere. Those who had the money moved inland. Many Germans migrated to Pennsylvania, while a large number of Scandinavians moved onto the Great Plains.

There was a huge demand for workers to help build bridges, canals, and railroads. Beginning about 1820, immigrants started to arrive in hordes, and their numbers increased each year. In 1825, 10,000 came, and five years later, almost 24,000. A whopping 300,000 arrived in 1849, the majority coming from Ireland as a result of the potato-crop failure. So many Irish immigrated that New York City, in time, came to have a larger Irish population than Dublin!

From *Everyday Life: Immigration* © Good Year Books.

Although many Irish found employment building canals and working on the eastern half of the transcontinental railroad, most stayed in the coastal cities along the Atlantic. The reason they did not move elsewhere was a matter of economics. They were too poor to buy either supplies or railroad tickets to seek their fortunes inland.

So they mostly stayed in the large cities, where they faced prejudice and discrimination almost from the beginning. The Irish were singled out for hatred for two reasons: they were poor and they were Catholic. Because they were poor, they accepted any kind of work at the lowest wage. This created resentment on the part of other workers, who felt their jobs were in jeopardy from such an influx of unskilled labor. Mobs often attacked and beat up Irish laborers whom they felt were taking jobs away from them.

Since most of the other immigrants to America were Protestants, the Irish also suffered because of their religion. Notices were tacked to the doors and gates of factories and businesses that read "Irish Need Not Apply!" Anti-Catholicism was preached by such groups as the Know-Nothing Party, whose name came from its members being sworn to answer "I know nothing" when questioned about anything. Hatred ran so deep that a bigoted newspaper of the day once printed a Know-Nothing menu that included such entrees as "Roasted Catholic" and "Broiled Priest."

A Know-Nothing political cartoon accusing Irish and German immigrants of stealing elections and running big-city political machines.

In spite of hardships and, as in the case of the Irish, extreme prejudice, most immigrants succeeded in making a new life for themselves in America. Their children attended public schools and quickly became "Americanized." In time, they made valuable contributions in art, science, and other fields. Some became quite prosperous, and a few, such as steel-industry tycoon Andrew Carnegie, even became millionaires!

It has been said that America is a nation of immigrants. This statement might even be applied to Native Americans, whom historians believe migrated from Asia across the Bering Straits of Alaska centuries ago. All of us then, with the exception of recent arrivals, are descendants of immigrants who risked everything for a chance at a better life in America. To these brave and hardy people, we should forever be indebted.

From *Everyday Life: Immigration* © Good Year Books.

Name _____ Date _____

Write a Letter About Life in America

Imagine yourself an immigrant who has been in America for six months. Write a letter to a friend in your native land in which you try to persuade her or him to emigrate. Give reasons why you think such a move would be wise.

March 5, 1835

Dear _____,

_____

_____

_____

_____

_____

_____

_____

_____

_____

_____

_____

_____

_____

_____

_____

_____

_____

_____

_____

Your friend,

_____

From *Everyday Life: Immigration* © Good Year Books.

Name _____ Date _____

Brush Up on Your European Geography

Most people who immigrated to the United States between the years 1820 and 1880 came from western Europe. They came from such places as England, Scotland, Ireland, Switzerland, the German states, and the Scandinavian countries.

How familiar are you with the nations of western Europe today? Consult an encyclopedia, an atlas, or some other source, and answer the questions at the right.

1. What four countries or parts of countries make up the United Kingdom of Great Britain, and what are their capitals?

   _____

   _____

   _____

2. The Republic of Ireland was also a part of the United Kingdom until 1919, when it became an independent nation. The capital of the Irish Republic is _____.

3. List the three Scandinavian countries and their capitals.

   _____

   _____

   _____

4. Finland is not considered one of the Scandinavian countries, but Finns were included among the many immigrants of the Old Immigration period. What is Finland's capital?

   _____

5. When we speak of immigrants coming from Germany in the early 1800s, we are incorrect. Instead of a unified Germany, there were a number of independent German states. In what year did these states unite and form one nation? _____

6. Some immigrants during the Old Migration came from Switzerland. Switzerland is located amid some of western Europe's highest mountains, the famous _____.

Name _____ Date _____

Bake a Batch of Scottish Crumblies

Immigrants who came to America during the Old Immigration brought their ideas and ways of doing things with them. These included recipes for their favorite foods and desserts.

You are probably familiar with such foreign dishes as Swedish meatballs, Irish stew, and English plum pudding. But there are many others, some of which are easy to prepare.

At the right is a recipe for making crumblies, a favorite cookie of the Scots. With the help of an adult, you can bake four dozen of these delicious cookies in 20 minutes.

Here are the ingredients you will need:

1 1/3 cups of brown sugar

1 cup butter or margarine

1/4 tsp. nutmeg

1/4 tsp. salt

2 cups white flour

Here is what you do:

1. Blend the brown sugar and butter or margarine into a cream.

2. Add the nutmeg and salt.

3. Combine the mixture with flour, working it in with your hands.

4. Roll the dough to a thickness of about 1/3 inch.

5. Cut the dough into 1 1/2 inch squares.

6. Place the squares on a cookie sheet greased with butter or margarine, or in a pan lined with greased aluminum foil.

7. Bake at 375°F for 20 minutes.

8. Serve.

From Everyday Life: Immigration © Good Year Books.

Name _____ Date _____

Distinguish Between Sentences and Fragments

Can you tell when a statement is a complete sentence and not just a fragment? Fragments are statements that lack either a verb or a subject or do not express a complete thought. Authors sometimes use fragments in writing, but, as a student, you should be careful to always write in complete sentences.

At the right are nine statements. Some are fragments, while others are complete sentences. On the line to the left of each, write **F** if the statement is a fragment or **S** if it is a complete sentence. Lines are provided for you to make complete sentences of those statements you think are fragments.

1. _____ Almost two million immigrants from England and Ireland.
_____

2. _____ The Old Immigration occurred between 1820 and 1880.
_____

3. _____ When the Irish potato crop failed.
_____

4. _____ Many immigrants from Germany.
_____

5. _____ Runners and others took advantage of emigrants.
_____

6. _____ Where jobs were plentiful and land was cheap.
_____

7. _____ Most newly arrived immigrants stayed in northeastern cities.
_____

8. _____ Because they were Catholic, the Irish faced discrimination and hostility.
_____

9. _____ Because the Irish were poor.
_____

From Everyday Life: Immigration ©Good Year Books.

CHAPTER 4

Crossing the Ocean

Imagine yourself on a sailing ship coming to America in the year 1830. The weather has been unusually rough, as the small ship has encountered one storm after another. You are seasick; your parents, brothers, and sisters are seasick; everyone, it seems, is seasick. The odor is unbearable, but you do not have the energy to care. Day after day you lie almost motionless on your bunk. You ask yourself: "Will this terrible voyage ever end?"

Almost every immigrant who came to America in the 1800s and early 1900s could relate to the above story. This was especially true during the days of the sailing ship. A ship powered by sail usually took about forty days to make the Atlantic crossing. Often this time was greatly extended if the weather was bad or the winds unfavorable. Voyages of up to six months were not uncommon.

An immigrant ship sinks after running aground off Nova Scotia on April 1, 1873. From a lithograph by Currier and Ives.

Early emigrant voyages were also dangerous. During one year in the 1830s, seventeen ships sank on the Liverpool to Quebec (Canada) run alone. Between 1847 and 1853, fifty-nine immigrant ships went down. Sometimes ships were lost in heavy weather because they were old and overcrowded. Others sank after fires broke out because of carelessness on the part of the crew or passengers.

As though the dangers of the voyage were not enough, emigrants also had to contend with disease. Typhus, cholera, measles, dysentery, smallpox, and yellow fever killed thousands of emigrants before they ever reached America. Until the middle of the 1800s, the death rate on immigrant ships approached 20 percent. Sometimes entire families died at sea, and their bodies were thrown overboard. On any given ship, half the children might die of measles or some other contagious disease, while on others, the majority of one nationality might perish. An immigrant ship named *The April* reported the deaths of five-hundred Germans on one Atlantic crossing in the 1840s.

Why was disease so rampant on early voyages? Passengers did undergo a physical examination before boarding, but it amounted to little more than a farce (joke). One doctor might examine as many as 400 emigrants in a period of two hours. That equals 200 each hour, or about 3 persons a minute. Such a quick inspection allowed only enough time to check tongues and pulses.

From *Everyday Life: Immigration* ©Good Year Books.

Emigrants were never required to remove their clothes and hats, which meant that many diseases or conditions went undetected. There was no way of knowing if someone had lice or was infected with a rash or body sores.

Many ships in the early part of the 1800s had no doctors aboard. Emigrants on those vessels were left to fend for themselves when they became ill. Those ships that could boast of a doctor often had someone with little more training than a pharmacist. Sometimes the doctor's medical knowledge came solely from having thumbed through a single manual. Yet these "doctors" prescribed medicine and performed surgery!

Even if the weather was pleasant and disease was at a minimum, an early Atlantic crossing still posed hardships for emigrants.

Emigrants from eastern Europe relax and soak up the sun on the deck of a ship bringing them to America in 1902.

This was because they were confined to the lower part of the ship, called steerage. Until steamships came into use in the 1840s and 1850s, the steerage section of a sailing ship was uncomfortably small. It was usually about seventy-five feet long, twenty-five feet wide, and five feet high. Two rows of bunks on either side formed an aisle down the middle. Bunks were crammed into box-like partitions ten feet wide, five feet long, and less than three feet high. Into these small quarters from six to ten people were expected to exist for forty days or more!

Some sailing ships had no washrooms for steerage passengers. Those that did might have only one for every one hundred persons. Men and women often shared the same facility, which made for a lot of embarrassment on the part of everyone. Other ships had bathrooms for women only, with men having to go above deck.

A typical ship's washroom might contain, besides a toilet, up to ten sinks. Sometimes the faucets in the sinks were broken and did not work. When they did work, they ran only cold, salty water. Emigrants used the sinks for all their needs. They not only bathed at them but washed their dirty dishes and clothes in them as well. Since nothing resembling cleanser was available, the sinks stayed greasy and grimy during the entire Atlantic crossing.

From *Everyday Life: Immigration* ©Good Year Books.

Relieved that their long voyage is finally over, excited immigrants catch their first glimpse of the Statue of Liberty.

Emigrants had to use the sinks to wash pots and dishes because on most early sailing ships they cooked their own food. Those who were wise and had the means always brought extra food with them. Food provided by the shipping line might consist of only stale biscuits, cold soup, boiled potatoes, and stringy beef. There was never enough to go around and never enough to satisfy one's hunger. Only emigrants who had money or whiskey to bribe the cooks ate well and went to bed with full stomachs.

Not all emigrant voyages during the days of sailing ships were marked by such extreme hardships. As mentioned before, some voyages, when the weather was nice and the seas calm, were even pleasant. Much also depended on the captain and the crew. Some captains were kindhearted and treated their passengers well. They permitted no cruelty on the part of their crews, and they allowed steerage passengers to go up on deck for fresh air and relaxation. They made every attempt to feed emigrants as well as possible and to see to their comfort. Contrast this to the situation on some ships, where crew members regularly beat steerage passengers, and cooks served them coffee made of salt water!

Emigrant voyages improved considerably with the introduction of the steamship in the 1840s. By the end of the 1870s, the price of a steerage ticket had fallen to about $12, and this included food. The overall treatment of passengers by captains and crews also improved.

But the main advantage of steam over sail was in the length of the voyage. A steamship could make the Atlantic crossing in ten days or less. To have the crossing time reduced from forty days to ten days or less must have seemed like a miracle to those steamship passengers who had made earlier voyages in sailing ships.

Even with faster travel and better food, an Atlantic crossing was still far from a picnic. Conditions in steerage remained as crowded as ever, and seasickness posed a never-ending problem. Added to this were the differences

From Everyday Life: Immigration ©Good Year Books.

in nationalities on later voyages. Unlike the Old Immigration, when most immigrants came from northern and western Europe, those who came during the New Immigration (starting around 1880) came mostly from southern and eastern Europe. There were Greeks, Italians, Ukrainians, and Jews. There were Russians, Poles, Lithuanians, Hungarians, and other nationalities. Mix these with emigrants who continued to come from northern and western Europe, and a language barrier is rather obvious. The inability to understand one another made Atlantic crossings during this period difficult for all concerned.

Immigrants on their way to Ellis Island for processing crowd the deck of the *S.S. Patricia* in New York harbor in 1906.

But emigrant voyages often had a brighter side, too. In spite of the miseries associated with traveling in steerage, emigrants still managed to have fun on steamships. During good weather, they were allowed to come up on deck, even at night. There they talked, read, played cards, danced, and shared their dreams of America. Children played games and had a chance to forget, at least for a short time, their cramped and uncomfortable existence below deck.

Language proved no problem when it came to such recreation as dancing. All that was required for a dance to begin was for an emigrant to have an accordion or some other musical instrument. Regardless of the language of a particular song, people could still hum along and clap their hands to the beat of the music. Young couples of different nationalities danced together for hours without understanding a word the other was saying.

The sufferings endured during the Atlantic crossing were quickly forgotten when emigrants heard someone shout "Land!" They rushed to the ship's rails to catch a first glimpse of the country they would soon call their own. Old and young alike gazed admiringly at the Statue of Liberty, tears streaming down their faces. Some people cried; others shouted. Some hugged everyone in sight and danced jigs. Many fell to their knees and gave thanks. At long last, their terrible ordeal was over.

Name _____ Date _____

Fill In a Venn Diagram

Fill in the Venn diagram below to compare an immigrant crossing of the Atlantic Ocean during the Old and New Immigration periods. Write facts about each in the appropriate place. List features common to both where the circles overlap.

Old Immigration

Both

New Immigration

Name _____ Date _____

Interpret a Poem About the Statue of Liberty

Inscribed (written) on the pedestal on which the Statue of Liberty stands is a poem by Emma Lazarus, an American poet who lived from 1849 to 1887. The last lines of the poem read:

"Keep ancient lands, your storied pomp," cries she

With silent lips. "Give me your tired, your poor,

Your huddled masses yearning to breathe free,

The wretched refuse of your teeming shore,

Send these, the homeless, tempest-tost to me,

I lift my lamp beside the golden door!"

On the lines provided, write your interpretation of what this last part of Emma Lazarus's poem means.

_____

_____

_____

_____

_____

_____

_____

_____

_____

_____

_____

_____

_____

Name _____ Date _____

Solve an Immigration Puzzle

Fill in the sentences at the bottom of the page and complete each word in the puzzle below. The sentences are based on the reading.

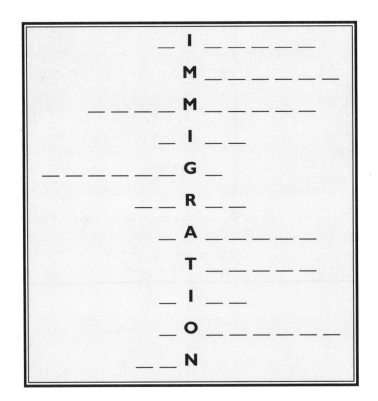

1. Emigrants were excited when they first saw the Statue of _____.

2. _____ was a disease that took the lives of many emigrant children on Atlantic crossings.

3. _____ began to replace sailing ships in the middle of the 1800s.

4. The steerage area on sailing ships was no more than twenty-five feet _____.

5. The part of a ship where most emigrant passengers stayed was called _____.

6. A sailing ship usually took about _____ days to cross the Atlantic.

7. _____ was a form of recreation in which language was no barrier.

8. By the late 1870s, the price of a steerage ticket had fallen to _____ dollars.

9. Sailing ships were powered by the _____.

10. Most immigrants during the Old Immigration came from _____ and western Europe.

11. A steamship could cross the Atlantic Ocean in _____ days or less.

From Everyday Life: Immigration © Good Year Books.

Name _____ Date _____

Research and Answer Questions About Typhus

You have learned that immigrants brought a variety of contagious diseases on board ships in the days of the Old Immigration. Physical examinations were hurried and incomplete, resulting in cholera, smallpox, measles, and typhus spreading rapidly throughout the steerage section of immigrant ships. Of these, typhus was the worst. In 1847 alone, more than 7,000 emigrants died of typhus while crossing the Atlantic. Typhus was so prevalent that it came to be called the "ship's disease."

Read about typhus in an encyclopedia or other book, and answer the questions to the right.

1. What is typhus, and what causes it?

_____

_____

2. What are the symptoms of typhus?

_____

_____

3. In addition to outbreaks on immigrant ships, what are some other places or times in history when typhus epidemics have occurred?

_____

_____

4. What simple measures can be taken to prevent typhus?

_____

_____

5. How is typhus treated?

_____

_____

6. What method was formerly used to prevent outbreaks of typhus among refugees and displaced persons during time of war?

_____

_____

_____

_____

CHAPTER 5

Coming in the Third Wave

Between 1880 and the beginning of the Great Depression in 1929, millions upon millions of new immigrants arrived in America. Some estimates place the number as high as 20 million. Most were from southern and eastern Europe, and the period in which they came is referred to as the New Immigration. It represented the third great wave of immigration to America.

Constantine Panunzio from Italy was typical of these later arrivals, and the problems he faced were typical of those who came at that time. Knowing no English, he went from job to job, trying to make a living in an alien country. Sometimes he was fired from jobs because he got involved in fights between immigrants of different nationalities. When he finally settled in, working on a farm in Maine, he was twenty years old.

Even at the age of twenty, Constantine was determined to get an education. While still working on the farm, he enrolled in school for the first time. Can you imagine the humiliation he suffered? Students as young as six years old teased and tormented him because of his age and his inability to speak English. But Constantine, unlike many immigrants, survived the taunts and insults and succeeded quite well in school. He even went on to obtain a college degree.

Just as typical as Constantine Panunzio were those immigrants who experienced failure or disappointment in their adopted land. Their numbers were far greater than those who truly found the American Dream. One such person was Josef Leksa, a Slovak immigrant who fled from the old Austro-Hungarian Empire that ruled a large part of central Europe until the end of World War I.

Josef Leksa came to America at the age of nineteen filled with hopes and dreams of a new life. He found work in a coal mine and thought his future was secure. But then disaster struck. He was nearly killed in an accident deep in the mine, and his injuries left him maimed for life. While recovering in the hospital, he signed a paper he could not read that was presented to him by the mining company's lawyer. He thought the paper guaranteed him a large sum of money to compensate for his crippling injuries.

An 1873 advertising circular promotes land in Iowa and Nebraska. Such circulars enticed many immigrants to settle on the Plains in the late 1800s.

From *Everyday Life: Immigration* © Good Year Books.

Josef Leksa was mistaken. Upon leaving the hospital on crutches, he went immediately to the mining company's office to collect his payment. Was he ever shocked! By signing a paper he did not understand, he had agreed to accept a mere $200 for almost being killed in the company's mine. Like many immigrants, Josef had been taken advantage of because he knew no English.

Every immigrant who came to America during the New Immigration could tell a story similar to that of Josef Leksa or Constantine Panunzio. Italians, Greeks, Poles, Slovaks, Russians, Ukrainians, Czechs, Hungarians, Lithuanians, Bulgarians, and other nationalities were all oftentimes mocked and taken advantage of at every turn.

Millions who came in this third wave were Jews. Unlike other immigrants at the time who felt they could always return to their homelands if things did not work out in America, Jewish arrivals came to stay. They had no other choice. Most had fled Europe to escape pogroms, or persecutions, and to return might risk certain death.

Golda Meir, once a Jewish immigrant from Russia, served as Prime Minister of Israel from 1969 to 1974.

One Jewish immigrant who fled from persecution was a little girl named Golda Meir. You may have heard of her; if not, you will surely read about her at some point in your study of history. Golda came to America from Russia in 1906 with her mother and sisters. (Her father had emigrated earlier.) She grew up, married, and emigrated from the United States to Palestine in 1921. Like many other Jews, she worked hard for the establishment of a Jewish nation. That nation—Israel—became a reality in 1948. Twenty-one years later, Golda became the Prime Minister of the very country she helped create.

Golda Meir's family came to America for the same reason that others of her faith came: to escape the pogroms that were characteristic of much of Europe at the time. During pogroms, mobs ran uncontrolled through towns and rural areas, killing Jews. What were the police in those areas doing when such massacres occurred? At times, nothing. Police and soldiers often stood by and watched as helpless people were murdered before their eyes. Sometimes, as you learned previously, the police and soldiers took part in the killings themselves.

Whereas millions of Jews emigrated to America to escape religious persecution, other eastern Europeans came because of uprisings or political discontent in their homelands. Many had been members of secret revolutionary groups singled out by the police for their activities and had to flee for their lives.

Other people simply gave up on waiting for their governments to carry out reforms that would make their lives easier. They had tried petitioning their rulers in person, only to be met by police and soldiers under orders to turn back all demonstrators.

One terrible incident that occurred in Russia in 1905 illustrates the point well. On January 22 of that year, several hundred thousand poor people marched toward the Winter Palace in St. Petersburg to present Czar Nicholas II with a petition. The petition begged the Czar to help them. It told of the misery and the hunger experienced by the peasants and the working class of Russia. At no point was the crowd threatening or unruly. Nearly everyone, in fact, carried either a portrait of the Czar or a banner singing his praises.

Nicholas II was not even at the palace. He was staying at another palace outside the city at the time. But it mattered little; his soldiers were there. They fired into the crowd and charged them with drawn sabers (swords). Nearly 1,500 innocent people were killed, including many women and children.

Troops of Czar Nicholas II charge peaceful demonstrators on Bloody Sunday, January 22, 1905. More than 1,000 men, women, and children were killed.

Similar incidents occurred elsewhere in eastern Europe, causing millions to pack up and leave for America. By and large, the vast majority of immigrants who came to America during the New Immigration were poor peasants who had come to believe that their lives would never change in their native lands.

Beginning in the late 1880s, people from all over eastern and southern Europe flocked to port cities in western Europe. Along the way they were harassed and sometimes robbed by border guards. The wisest sewed money into the linings of their coats to ensure that they had something left when they boarded ship.

Many poor families sent their children to America alone. Such was the case of a Romanian Jewish family with a boy named

From *Everyday Life: Immigration* ©Good Year Books.

Marcus Ravage. Marcus came to America in 1900 as a teenager. His aged parents were in no position to uproot their lives and emigrate, so they saved their money and sent their only son instead.

Marcus Ravage's mother knew she would never see her son again once he left his village. But in the months prior to his departure, she worked hard to make his journey as comfortable and as safe as possible. She baked delicious treats for him to carry and mended all of his clothes. She replaced lost buttons and made him new underwear. Into the lining of his coat she sewed, as did most mothers with a son or daughter leaving for America, several gold coins in case he encountered robbers or greedy border guards along the way.

You will recall that immigrants who came to America during the Old Immigration were, except for the Irish, mostly Protestants. They were farmers and skilled laborers who arrived at a time when additional laborers were desperately needed in America. Immigrants who came in the late 1800s and early 1900s were different. They were almost all Catholics, Jews, or members of the Eastern Orthodox Church. They looked different and dressed unlike earlier immigrants, and they spoke "strange-sounding" languages. You can guess who probably resented their presence the most: Americans who had themselves been immigrants only a few years before. The main complaint of these "older Americans" was that the newcomers took away jobs and caused wages to remain low.

The huge influx of newcomers to America during this time caused many people to demand that their government place restrictions on immigration. Congress complied, beginning in 1882 with the Chinese Exclusion Act. This act barred any future Chinese from entering the country. (The story of the Chinese and the hostility they faced on the West Coast will be covered in Chapter 7.) In the years that followed, Congress also established quotas that limited the number of people who could immigrate yearly to America from other countries. In so doing, America slammed the door on unrestricted immigration, which had been its policy for over a hundred years.

A political cartoon of 1893 makes it clear that all nationalities are welcome in America's "school" except the Chinese.

Name _____ Date _____

Participate in a Skit
(A Teacher-Directed Activity)

Divide the class into four groups. Each group should choose one of the skits listed. Students should use their imagination and creative skills in planning their skit. Each skit should be about five minutes in length.

Any student in a group not participating directly in a skit can either help make simple props or critique skits and rate them at the conclusion of the activity. There is a lead-in to each skit to help students in their planning.

Skit 1—A Brother and Sister from a Village in Eastern Europe Leave Their Aged Parents to Emigrate to America

Scenes of family members leaving others behind to come to America were commonplace throughout eastern and southern Europe. Sometimes it was the father who emigrated alone; at other times it was a son or a daughter, or perhaps both. Create this scene around the heart-rending moment when a brother and sister take leave of their parents.

Skit 2—A Peasant Family Debates the Pros and Cons of Emigrating

For some, whether to leave their homeland and go to a strange, new country was not an easy decision to make. Should they go? Should they stay? Was life in America any better for poor, uneducated peasants than it was in their village? At least, in their village, they were among their own kind. Would it be the same in America?

Create this skit involving all members of a peasant family discussing what they should do.

Skit 3—A Family Sees One of Its Members Turned Back at a Medical Station Because He or She Has Symptoms of Cholera

Unlike immigrants who came to America during the Old Immigration, those who came later were subjected to rigorous physical exams in European port cities before being allowed to board ship. Many failed and were sent back to their native villages.

Can you imagine the heartbreak of a family upon seeing one of its members rejected for medical reasons and left behind while the others sailed away to a new life? Create this skit around such a scene.

Skit 4—An Immigrant Youngster's First Day at School in America

Immigrant schoolchildren were often teased and harassed by their classmates. Create this skit around what an immigrant child's first day at school might have been like.

From Everyday Life: Immigration © Good Year Books.

Name _____ Date _____

Give Your Thoughts on Prejudice

You have learned that millions of Jews immigrated to the United States during the period of the New Immigration. They came because they suffered terrible persecution in Russia and in other eastern European countries.

Although Jewish immigrants did not need to worry about pogroms in America, they did encounter much prejudice and discrimination. So did other immigrants who came to our country at the same time.

What causes prejudice? Is it a learned attitude? Can it be prevented? Give your best answers to these and the other questions at the right.

1. What is prejudice?

_____

_____

_____

2. What do you think are the underlying causes of prejudice?

_____

_____

_____

3. Do you consider yourself prejudiced? Why or why not?

_____

_____

_____

4. Is prejudice a learned attitude? Explain your answer.

_____

_____

_____

5. In your opinion, can prejudice be prevented, or do you think it will exist forever? Explain your answer.

_____

_____

6. Which groups in America still experience prejudice today?

_____

_____

_____

Name _____ Date _____

Find the Mean, Mode, and Range

In the box are immigration statistics for each decade of the New Immigration period. Round each figure to the nearest million and answer the questions at the right. You may need to refer to your mathematics textbook for a quick review of *mean*, *mode*, and *range*, as well as of *median*.

Years	Number of Immigrants
1880–1890	5,687,564
1891–1900	3,687,564
1901–1910	8,795,386
1911–1920	5,735,811
1921–1930	4,107,209

1. With all figures rounded to the nearest million, what was the total number of immigrants between 1880 and 1930? _____

2. No median is represented in the immigration figures. Can you explain why?_____

3. There are two modes represented in the figures. They are _____ and _____.

4. What is the mean number of immigrants? Use the space below to figure your answer. The mean is _____

5. What is the range? _____

From Everyday Life: Immigration © Good Year Books.

Name _____ Date _____

Use Context Clues to Complete Sentences

Fill in the blanks in the sentences using the words in the box. Use each word only once.

additional	eastern	located	population
born	flow	native	receiving
center	immigrant	next	replaced
currency	landed	obtain	turn

In 1900, the _____ of the United States was 76 million. Of this number, more than 10 million had been _____ in Europe. More than twice this number were born in America of _____ parents. These figures show how large the _____ of immigrants was at the _____ of the century.

Seven of every ten immigrants who came to America during the New Immigration were from southern and _____ Europe. All of these arrived and were processed at the immigration _____ on Ellis Island in New York. But, until 1855, there was no Ellis Island nor any other _____ station in New York. Immigrants coming to America in the early 1800s _____ at such seaports as Boston, Philadelphia, Baltimore, and New Orleans.

The first immigrant-receiving station in New York was in an old fort called Castle Garden. Castle Garden was _____ at the tip of Manhattan Island, the principal port of New York City. It served both as a receiving center and as a protective haven for new arrivals. At Castle Garden, immigrants could _____ information on lodging and travel tickets and exchange their foreign _____ for U.S. dollars.

Castle Garden was the main immigrant-processing center until it was _____ by Ellis Island in 1892. Ellis Island, though it also offered protection to immigrants, was established with an _____ purpose in mind. That purpose was to screen out "undesirables" and ship them back to their _____ lands.

You will learn about Ellis Island in the _____ chapter.

CHAPTER 6

Arriving at Ellis Island

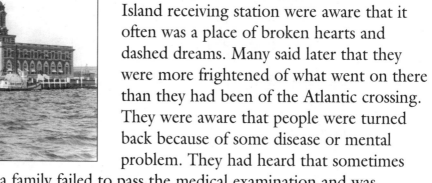

nzia Yezierska's anticipation was no different from other immigrants on her ship when they arrived in New York in 1901. She was giddy with excitement. The sight of America and the Statue of Liberty in the harbor must have brought tears to her eyes. The young Russian girl later wrote that people hugged and danced when they first caught sight of their adopted land. Old men and old women, she related, had "in their eyes a look of young people in love."

Anzia Yezierska's description of how immigrants reacted upon seeing the Statue of Liberty was true of every ship that arrived in the harbor. But the elation and excitement were tempered (lessened) somewhat by what still lay ahead: Ellis Island.

As you learned in Chapter 5, Ellis Island replaced Castle Garden as the main U.S. immigration center in 1892. Before it closed in 1954, more than 16 million immigrants had passed through its gates. Each of these could probably relate stories similar to the ones that follow.

Ellis Island in New York harbor, which for 62 years was the main immigrant-processing center in the United States.

Immigrants who arrived at the Ellis Island receiving station were aware that it often was a place of broken hearts and dashed dreams. Many said later that they were more frightened of what went on there than they had been of the Atlantic crossing. They were aware that people were turned back because of some disease or mental problem. They had heard that sometimes one member of a family failed to pass the medical examination and was immediately put on a ship and sent home. Sometimes this family member was a child. It made no difference. Children as young as ten were put on ships and sent back to fend for themselves. Can you imagine the heartbreak of the parents? And can you imagine the desperation that would drive some immigrants—turned back because of disease or disability—to jump into the river and try to swim to the mainland? Almost all of these poor souls drowned.

The long process of gaining entry into America began with a ferryboat ride from the ship to Ellis Island. When the immigrants left the ferry, they

From *Everyday Life: Immigration* ©Good Year Books.

were hurried into a large room called the Registry Room, or the Great Hall. They were rushed to the point that they had little time to take in their surroundings. *Hurry. Stay in line. Move quicker. Don't stand there, stand here. Don't poke around; we don't have all day.* The commands were endless—and frightening.

In the Registry Room, immigrants were separated into groups of thirty. The first ordeal they faced was the medical examination. Although it probably seemed to these worried newcomers that this took a lifetime, the examination was usually over in less than five minutes. The immigrants formed a line and passed between two doctors. One doctor checked for signs of any physical or mental disability. The other was on the lookout for contagious diseases. Any immigrant suspected of having some shortcoming was marked with white chalk and detained for further examination.

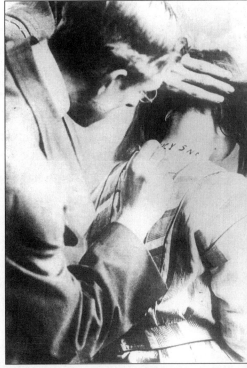

An immigration official prints an immigrant's name on the back of her neck in indelible ink.

The medical examiners particularly checked for trachoma, a contagious eye disease that can cause blindness. Anyone thought to have trachoma had *CT* chalked on his or her clothing. Many immigrants were denied admission because they were detected with this dread disease.

There was a chalked letter for everything. People with heart problems had *H* chalked on their coats or shirts. Those with a hernia received a *K*, while anyone having a scalp infection was given the letters *Sc*. People who were crippled in any way were marked with an *L*.

Probably the most dreaded mark was *X*. An *X* implied that the immigrant had a mental disorder, a condition that resulted in immediate deportation. Sometimes immigrants who were simply nervous or frightened were deemed mentally unfit and sent back to Europe. Such nearly happened to one young girl, who was so nervous upon arrival at Ellis Island that she developed warts on her hands. A doctor chalked an *X* on her coat, and her family thought she would certainly be detained. But some kind gentleman, whether another immigrant or perhaps even an inspector is not known, suggested that she turn her coat inside out to hide the chalk mark. She did and was allowed to pass through.

From *Everyday Life: Immigration* ©Good Year Books.

Intelligence tests given to immigrants suspected of having mental disorders consisted of a variety of questions and activities. With an interpreter at hand, the examiner might ask a person to solve a number of math problems or work a puzzle. Sometimes he or she would be asked to count backwards or place wooden squares or circles in the appropriate places on a board. At other times the person being examined might be asked to interpret expressions on the faces of pictures shown them.

Sometimes immigrants failed intelligence tests simply because they viewed things differently from people in America. One part of a test given immigrant children offers a good example. The children were shown a picture of a boy digging a hole in the ground—a dead rabbit lying at his feet—and asked to interpret its meaning. It was common for immigrant children from Europe to reply that the boy had killed the rabbit to eat. But that was not the answer immigrant officials were looking for. The correct answer was that the dead rabbit was a family pet and that the boy had dug a hole to bury it. Do you think many immigrant children were sent back to Europe because they gave the wrong answer to such a foolish and unfair question?

Once immigrants had cleared all medical examinations, they next faced a list of questions from various immigration officials. Where did you come from? How much money do you have? Can you work? Do you have a skill? Do you have a job waiting for you? Do you have family here? Is someone meeting you? Do you already have a place to stay? Twenty or thirty questions were thrown at immigrants in a matter of a few minutes. They all realized that a wrong answer to any of them might result in their being sent back to Europe.

An inspector at Ellis Island checks an immigrant's eyes for trachoma. Anyone detected with trachoma faced the possibility of being sent back to Europe.

In spite of their fears, most immigrants were only at Ellis Island for a few hours. Those who passed all their examinations then boarded a ferry for the twenty-five minute ride to the mainland. About 30 percent of the new arrivals stayed in New York City. The others bought railroad tickets to other places. The vast majority stayed in the industrial cities of the northeast, but some moved on to destinations as far away as the states of California and Washington.

From *Everyday Life: Immigration* ©Good Year Books.

What about those immigrants who were detained for a few days, or even weeks? Ellis Island had been built to meet most of their needs. There were two kitchens that served hot meals in a large dining hall. One kitchen prepared regular meals, while the other cooked special foods required by people of the Jewish faith. And what meals they were to these poor immigrants accustomed to hunger and deprivation! Eggs with bread and butter for breakfast, washed down with either coffee or milk. And for dinner? The immigrants could not believe their eyes! Potatoes, vegetables, beef stew, soup, and perhaps a piece of fruit—and all at one sitting!

One of the dining halls at Ellis Island. Immigrants were surprised at the quality of food they were served at the receiving station.

Immigrant children were in awe of the special treats they sometimes received: fig bars, cookies, and ice cream, not to mention glasses of cold milk. And bananas! Most children, as well as their parents, had never seen a banana before they arrived at Ellis Island. At least one story survives of an immigrant eating a whole banana—skin and all—before being told he were supposed to peel it!

How did immigrants pass the time at Ellis Island? In the early days adults were limited to exercising on the roof of the main building. For children there was a small playground on the roof with tricycles, carts, and rocking horses. Beginning in 1914, however, many improvements were added that made the immigrants' stay on the island a little more enjoyable. They were allowed to use the lawns for exercise and play, and a number of activities and programs were started. A kindergarten kept youngsters occupied, while adults and older children could enjoy movies, concerts, and athletic contests.

Although recreational activities went far to lessen the fears and concerns of immigrants at Ellis Island, they did little to erase the unhappy memories the new arrivals carried with them when they left. Fiorello La Guardia, who later became mayor of New York City and who worked as an interpreter at the receiving station for a number of years, said he never grew accustomed to the despair and disappointment he saw daily. If someone who worked there felt that way, it is easy to imagine the anguish felt by the immigrants themselves.

A classroom for the children of immigrants temporarily detained at Ellis Island. Here children received valuable instruction that made their adjustment to life in America a little easier.

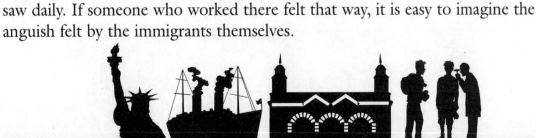

From Everyday Life: Immigration © Good Year Books.

Name _____ Date _____

Solve an Ellis Island Crossword

Across

3. _____ minutes, length of most medical exams at Ellis Island

4. _____ million, the number of immigrants processed at Ellis Island

6. Another name for the Registry Room

11. A contagious eye disease

12. Percent of immigrants who stayed in New York City

Down

1. Mayor La Guardia's first name

2. An *X* referred to this kind of disorder

3. Nineteen fifty-____, when Ellis Island closed

5. Fruit new to most immigrants

6. Castle _____

7. What a chalked *H* stood for

8. Statue of _____

9. Where Ellis Island was located

10. *Sc* implied this kind of infection

From *Everyday Life: Immigration* ©Good Year Books.

Name _____ Date _____

Make a Diary Entry

Imagine yourself an immigrant who has just stepped off the ferry from Ellis Island into the heart of New York City some time around the turn of the century. You gaze in disbelief at the tall buildings and at the hustle and bustle of the city streets. For the first time in your life, you see a trolley car and an elevated train. There is so much to see that your eyes cannot travel fast enough to take it all in.

On the lines, make a diary entry telling about your thoughts and your experiences on your first day in the big city.

May 10, 1900

Dear Diary,

_____
_____
_____
_____
_____
_____
_____
_____
_____
_____
_____
_____
_____
_____
_____
_____
_____
_____
_____
_____
_____
_____
_____

Name _____ Date _____

Solve These Ellis Island Word Problems

Here are four word problems dealing with the number of immigrants who were processed at Ellis Island. Solve each, and write its answer on the blank line. Space is provided for you to show your work.

1. Ellis Island was built to accommodate 5,000 immigrants daily. If an average of 2 percent were sent back to Europe, how many were sent back each day? _____ were sent back.

2. Five of every six immigrants passed through Ellis Island in a matter of hours. This meant that _____ percent were not detained or kept for further tests.

3. If 30 percent of the immigrants who cleared Ellis Island stayed in New York City, how many immigrants out of 5,000 took up residence in that city? _____ stayed in New York City.

4. Ellis Island operated as an immigrant-receiving station for 62 years. During that time, 16 million people passed through its gates. What was the average number to pass through each year? _____ each year.

From *Everyday Life: Immigration* ©Good Year Books.

Name _____ Date _____

Research a Nation of Southern or Eastern Europe

A majority of the immigrants who entered the United States through Ellis Island were from southern and eastern Europe. They came from many nations and regions, including Poland, Russia, Hungary, Greece, Italy, Lithuania, and the Ukraine.

Choose one of the above nations (or select another of your choice) and research it in an encyclopedia, almanac, or other book. Then answer the questions.

1. The name of the country on which I did research is _____.

2. My country's capital is _____.

3. The most recent population of my country is _____.

4. My country has a _____ form of government.

5. Other countries that border my country are _____.

6. _____, _____, and _____ are three important natural resources of my country.

7. The area of my country consists of _____ square miles.

8. Some chief agricultural products of my country are _____.

9. My country manufactures _____.

10. Some interesting places to visit in my country are _____.

11. Some favorite foods of my country are _____.

12. In my country, amusements and recreational activities include _____ _____.

From Everyday Life: Immigration © Good Year Books.

CHAPTER 7

Facing Hostility and Quotas

Even before the thirteen colonies won their independence from Great Britain, American reaction toward immigration was somewhat ambiguous (unclear and confusing).

On the one hand, immigrants were welcomed in a land that cried out for workers. Laborers were needed to clear the forests and to build roads and canals. They were needed to lay railroad track and to settle on farmland in the West. To get immigrants to come, railroads and other businesses placed ads in foreign newspapers. They tacked colorful posters on the walls of buildings. They promised good jobs and cheap land to all who would immigrate.

An anti-Jewish cartoon of 1892 shows New Yorkers leaving for the West as Jewish immigrants arrive from Russia. The wealthy Jewish man in the center holds blueprints for reconstructing New York.

But, although immigrants were encouraged to come, they were not so quickly accepted into the mainstream of American life. Many people saw them as second-class citizens and viewed them with distrust. Even a respected patriot like Benjamin Franklin, whom many considered the wisest man in America, was not above prejudice. Franklin worried that so many Germans were settling in Pennsylvania that the colony might fall under the control of "aliens." He was even concerned that German might become the official language of the United States when the colonies banded together to become a nation in 1776.

The first immigrants to face open hostility were the Irish. You may remember from Chapter 3 that a disastrous potato-crop failure in Ireland in 1845 caused thousands of starving peasants to emigrate to America. Here they joined a quarter-million other Irish who had arrived in the 1820s and 1830s. All told, more than two million Irish came to America during the period of the Old Immigration.

Why was so much prejudice directed against the Irish? The reason was primarily due to their religion. The vast majority of Americans were Protestants. The Irish were Catholics. Anti-Catholic feeling was so strong in

From *Everyday Life: Immigration* ©Good Year Books.

the United States that some people believed the Irish were sent here by the Pope to undermine American tradition and values. What is interesting is that the Irish, like other immigrants of the Old Immigration period, would later express strong feelings against newer arrivals who were Jewish, Greek Orthodox, or of other religious faiths.

Anti-Catholic sentiment in the 1850s was fanned by the Know-Nothing Party, to which you were introduced in Chapter 3. The real name of the Know-Nothings was the Order of the Star-Spangled Banner. Its members discriminated against anyone who was not white and Protestant. Later, the group would add African Americans and Jews to its list of people to hate.

After the Order of the Star-Spangled Banner faded away, another, more extreme organization arose, called the Ku Klux Klan. (Ku Klux was derived from the Greek word *kyklos*, which means "circle.") Actually, there was more than one Klan. The first appeared after the Civil War and directed its hatred against African Americans. It was a Southern-based group that ceased to exist in the 1870s.

A second Klan was organized in 1915. African Americans as well as Roman Catholics, Jews, foreigners, and anyone the Klan viewed as "radical" might be attacked and beaten up. So prevalent was "anti-foreign" feeling in the early 1900s that this second Klan

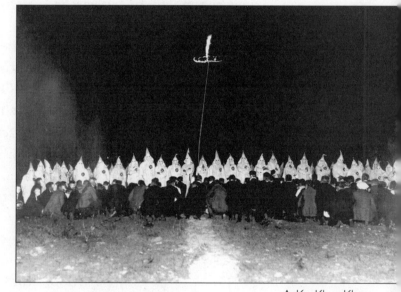

A Ku Klux Klan rally of the 1920s. By this time, the Klan had added Jews, Catholics, and foreigners to its hate list.

spread throughout the United States. Its was just as powerful in some northern states as it was in the South.

Although most Americans were never members of such organizations as the Ku Klux Klan, many nevertheless distrusted immigrants. Again, this was especially true of immigrants from southern and eastern Europe, as well as those from China. Why was this so?

Mention was made in Chapters 3 and 5 that immigrants took jobs that other Americans felt were rightfully theirs. Often immigrants would work at cheaper rates, which resulted in wages remaining low for all, causing even more resentment. Bosses added to the turmoil by sometimes firing all of their workers who had joined labor unions and replacing them with immigrants.

From Everyday Life: Immigration ©Good Year Books.

Immigrant workers were often caught up in strikes and labor disputes. It was not uncommon for a boss to mislead immigrants into believing they were being given regular jobs, when in reality they were being hired only as strikebreakers. Such deceit oftentimes resulted in brawls between immigrant workers and union workers out on strike.

But hatred toward immigrant groups had to do with more than just jobs. Later immigrants to America were distrusted simply because they were different. They dressed differently and they spoke different languages. They had different ways and they followed different religions. They stayed to themselves and congregated together in separate sections of America's cities.

Immigrants had little choice but to segregate themselves. They were pushed into slums, the poorest and drabbest of neighborhoods. Such areas in time became ghettos, places in which people of the same religion or racial origin are forced to live. Large cities on the East Coast had their *Little Italy*s and their *Little Poland*s. Those on the West Coast had their *Chinatown*s.

Every immigrant group faced hostility of some kind. Nearly all were ridiculed and discriminated against. Others were beaten, shot, and even lynched. However, the Chinese were the first immigrant group to be singled out by an act of Congress. The Chinese Exclusion Act of 1882 closed the door on further immigration from China. From 1882 until 1943, no additional Chinese were permitted to enter the United States.

Some Chinese had come to America during the Gold Rush of 1849. The majority, however, came at the time the transcontinental railroad was built. By 1880, more than 100,000 Chinese were living in America, most of them in California.

As was true of African Americans, the Chinese were victims of prejudice and hostility because they were of a different race. As such, their appearance and customs made them suspect among Americans who considered themselves native born. Chinese immigrants were mocked because they always worked in native costumes, and their men wore their hair in long queues, or pigtails. They were even resented because they took daily baths and ate such "un-Christian" foods as seaweed and mushrooms.

An 1886 advertisement for Magic Washer cleaning liquid. Its implication is that, with Magic Washer, Chinese labor is no longer needed.

From *Everyday Life: Immigration* ©Good Year Books.

Anti-Chinese sentiment often resulted in violence that led to the deaths of many innocent people. In 1885, for example, a mob in Rock Springs, Wyoming, killed twenty-eight Chinese and burned every Chinese home and business in the town.

Shortly after the Chinese Exclusion Act became law in 1882, Congress began to pass other legislation dealing with immigration. One law stated that criminals, paupers, and mentally ill immigrants could no longer come to America. Another required that immigrants had to pass a literacy test to gain admission. This last bill was rejected by three presidents, but it eventually became law over President Woodrow Wilson's veto in 1917.

World War I did much to heighten distrust of everything foreign. After the war, Americans opposed to unlimited immigration began to press Congress for tougher laws. Congress responded in 1921 with the Emergency Quota Act. This law established quotas, or fixed numbers of people, that could enter the United States from each country. The law was not fair. More immigrants could come from the northern and western parts of Europe than from the southern and eastern. And you will remember that Asians, especially Chinese, were not permitted to immigrate at all.

An anti-Chinese riot in Denver, Colorado, on October 31, 1880. Such outbreaks often resulted in the murder and the destruction of property of innocent Chinese immigrants.

The immigration law of 1921 was followed by others in 1924 and 1929. These new laws limited the number of immigrants who could enter the United States yearly to 150,000. By the time the Great Depression began in 1929, only a trickle of newcomers arrived annually at Ellis Island. America had closed the door on unrestricted immigration.

In spite of the fact that they were feared and mistrusted, immigrants who came during the New Immigration made lasting contributions to our nation. They helped build America's great cities and provided the labor for industries. They laid the railroad tracks that linked the nation together and helped settle the vast area of the Great Plains. Their children grew up to become leaders in all aspects of American life.

You will learn more about the contributions of immigrants in Chapter 10.

From Everyday Life: Immigration © Good Year Books.

Name _____ Date _____

Write Your Opinions About Immigration

You have learned that many people were opposed to our government's policy of unrestricted immigration, which continued well into the twentieth century. Even after quotas were established for all nations, some Americans continued to believe that immigration should be ended completely.

How do you personally feel about immigration—past and present? Write your opinions to the questions at right.

1. Should immigrants be required to pass a literacy test? Why or why not?

_____

_____

_____

2. Was it fair for the government to permit entry of more immigrants from northern and western Europe than from other areas? Why or why not? What does this preference indicate about public opinion at the time?

_____

_____

_____

3. Do you agree that limits should continue to be placed on immigration? If so, should every nation be allotted the same number of immigrants? Why or why not?

_____

_____

_____

4. Why do you think early immigrants referred to themselves as settlers or colonists but called those who came after 1880 *immigrants*?

_____

_____

_____

From Everyday Life: Immigration © Good Year Books.

Name _____ Date _____

Finish a Story

Here is a story that has been started for you. It is based on the experiences of a Ukrainian family trying to make their way from New York to the coal mines of western Pennsylvania in the 1880s. The beginning of the story is true, although the names used are fictitious. Add onto the story, and give it any ending you desire. You may continue on a separate sheet of paper if necessary.

Andrei Kostenko was ecstatic. He and his family had passed all their tests at Ellis Island and now stood on a street in Manhattan. All that remained was for the agent from the mining company to show up and provide them with tickets for their journey inland.

Andrei had been promised a job in a coal mine in Luzerne County, Pennsylvania. He, his wife Olga, and little daughter Rada were anxious to be on their way. While they waited for the agent, they chatted happily about the new life that they were about to begin.

All day long they waited. They waited throughout the night and into the next day. The agent from the mining company never appeared. Having no other course open to them, the Kostenkos picked up their baggage and started walking in the direction of Pennsylvania.

_____

_____

_____

_____

_____

_____

_____

_____

_____

_____

_____

_____

_____

_____

Name _____ Date _____

Make False Statements True

All of the statements below are false. Change the word(s) in italics to make them true. Write the replacement words(s) on the lines following the statements.

1. Benjamin Franklin worried that *Irish* might become the official language of the United States. _____

2. Benjamin Franklin is associated with the colony of *New York*. _____

3. The *Italians* were the first immigrants to feel the brunt of American hostility. _____

4. "Know-Nothings" was another name for the *Ku Klux Klan*. _____

5. The first Ku Klux Klan was organized after the *Revolutionary War*. _____

6. A second Ku Klux Klan founded in *1870* directed its activities against Jews, Catholics, and other minorities as well as African Americans. _____

7. The Irish who immigrated to America were *Protestants*. _____

8. A *revolution* in their country caused many Irish to emigrate in 1845.
   _____

9. The words *Ku Klux* came from the Greek word *kyklos*, which means "power."
   _____

10. *Colonies* are places where people of the same religion or racial origin are often forced to live. _____

11. Any additional *Catholics* were barred from entering the United States by a law passed by Congress in 1882. _____

12. The Emergency Quota Act of 1921 gave preference to immigrants from *southern and eastern* Europe. _____

13. The majority of Chinese laborers came to the United States to work on the *Erie Canal*.
   _____

From Everyday Life: Immigration © Good Year Books.

Name _____ Date _____

Solve Some Immigration Word Problems

Here are problems having to do with immigration quotas and statistics. Solve each and write its answer on the appropriate line. Space is provided for you to show your work.

1. The Immigration Act of 1924 limited the number of European immigrants who could enter the United States to 150,000 annually. The act also established quotas that were based on the number of Americans who had come, or whose ancestors had come from each country previously. Thus, 85 percent of the 150,000 permitted to enter were from northern and western Europe. The remainder came from southern and eastern Europe.

a. How many immigrants could come from northern and western Europe each year? _____ immigrants

b. How many could enter from southern and eastern Europe? _____ immigrants

2. In 1910, the peak year of immigration, about 900,000 Europeans immigrated to the United States. Some 700,000 of these came from southern and eastern Europe. In round figures, what percent came from northern and western Europe?

_____ %

3. About 500,000 Europeans came to America in 1880, the first year of the New Immigration. Of this number, only 50,000 came from southern and eastern Europe. How many more came from these areas in 1910 than in 1880?

_____ more

CHAPTER 8

Living in Ghettos and Tenements

Children in a New York alley about the year 1888. Photographed by reformer Jacob Riis, the boys were believed to have been members of a street gang.

At some point in this book it would be nice to say that the immigrant's experience in America was a happy one. But for most it was not, especially for those who came at the turn of the twentieth century. Those immigrants had to deal with conditions for which they were ill-prepared to cope.

There were, to be sure, happy times. Immigrants had their churches and social organizations, and they printed their own newspapers. They drew comfort and strength from being around their own kind and from speaking their native languages. And they watched with pride as their children attended public schools and became more "Americanized" with each passing day.

But, overall, America did not turn out to be the "Garden of Eden" the immigrants had expected. Its streets were not paved with gold, as some had been led to believe. All Americans did not live in big houses and wear fancy clothes with lots of jewelry. All Americans did not ride around in expensive carriages (later automobiles) and attend gala parties. Some did, of course, but most did not.

In Chapter 6 you met Anzia Yezierska, the young Russian girl who immigrated in 1901. Anzia later became a writer and told of her experiences in an article entitled "How I Found America." She explained how the reality of living in the slums of a large city changed her image of her adopted country. She found narrow streets littered with garbage cans and filth. She smelled sickening odors coming from the windows of hot, crowded tenement buildings. She saw firsthand how poverty and misery gave rise to crime and the spread of disease. And she wondered what had happened to the "golden country of her dreams."

Michael Gold was a young Jewish boy who came to America at about the same time as Anzia Yezierska. He lived with his family in a crowded tenement in New York City. Like Anzia, he too became a writer. His description of life in a ghetto is typical of what most immigrant families had to endure in America's large cities.

Are you familiar with a tenement building? Such buildings at the time were built to accommodate as many people as possible. They had five or six

From *Everyday Life: Immigration* ©Good Year Books.

floors, and each floor was divided into several apartments. The apartments in turn were divided into a number of very small rooms. Sometimes nine or more people were crammed into each room. It was so crowded that some of them slept on the floor.

Like others who grew up in tenements, Michael Gold had little good to say about the tenement building in which he lived. Plaster fell continually from the walls. The stairs were broken and in need of repair. Pipes froze and burst in winter, and for days tenants had no water to drink. Each time the greedy and uncaring landlord came to collect the rent, he ignored the pleas of Michael's mother to make the necessary repairs. Michael later wrote that his mother had once muttered that she "wished that the landlord's false teeth would choke him to death!"

An immigrant family at home, photographed in 1912 by Lewis Hine. Note the closeness and the clutter typical of tenement living at the time.

If winter meant intense cold and broken pipes, summer brought its own kind of misery for immigrants. Sometimes, to escape the heat and smells of their rooms, families picked up their bedding and searched for other places to sleep. They could be seen wandering the streets at all hours of the night. Some made their way to parks; others sought relief at the docks. Most, however, slept on the roofs of their tenement buildings. When it rained, they grabbed their blankets and dashed back to their rooms. But there were always a few who were too tired and miserable to care. They just stayed out in the rain.

Whether it came from Anzia Yezierska or Michael Gold, or from such well-known social reformers as Jacob Riis and Lewis Hine, the description of life in an immigrant ghetto was always the same. Riis and Hine were particularly concerned about the children. Pictures show the sad looks on the dirty faces of children peering from tenement windows. They show children playing in narrow alleys and other places where the sun never penetrated. They show thin children who died much too early from hunger and disease.

As though poor health was not enough, many children suffered from neglect. Parents often had no choice but to leave them at home while they worked. Often these children were no more than babies and toddlers. Sometimes they were left in the care of a brother or sister who was not much older. Other times children were simply abandoned when their parents felt

From Everyday Life: Immigration © Good Year Books.

they could no longer care for them. It was not uncommon to find a child left with a note attached saying, "Please take care of Jimmy (or Mario, or Shenya, or Dmitri)." Older children were simply put out into the street to fend for themselves.

An immigrant family making suspenders in their apartment on New York's East Side. From a photograph by Lewis Hine.

Many families stayed together by working together. You have probably heard of piecework. Piecework is work paid for by the amount done rather than by the hours worked. Entire immigrant families huddled around tables making artificial flowers, cigars, and other products. Children as young as two and three worked alongside their parents and older brothers and sisters performing simple tasks. The faster a family worked, the more they produced and earned. The story of families who survived in this manner will be told in detail in Chapter 9.

Other families took in boarders to get by. A family of seven with four rooms might live in one and rent out the others. As many as eight boarders often occupied the three rented rooms. Can you imagine living this way? Can you imagine sharing your home or apartment with strangers? Can you imagine that in your tenement building there might be only one toilet and that it might be located in the basement? Could you have coped with such a complete lack of privacy?

Some buildings were even more cramped. This was especially true of those occupied by immigrants known as Birds of Passage. Birds of Passage were men who came to America with no intention of staying. They only wanted to earn a certain amount of money and then return to their homelands. Using as few funds as possible for housing, they often shared unfurnished rooms. Sometimes as many as 13 or 14 men lived in one room, sleeping on the floor. Some of them even shared mattresses. Men who worked day shifts owned mattresses jointly with those who worked at night.

Deplorable living conditions were also the rule in cities and towns where steel mills, stockyards, and coal mines had sprung up. The story was always the same. Roofs leaked. Floors sagged. Cellars filled with water when it rained. Children played in mud and in the waste and trash from factories and mines.

From *Everyday Life: Immigration* © Good Year Books.

People got sick and died at alarming rates. And the factory and mine owners who rented the houses often did nothing to help their miserable tenants.

Why were immigrants thrust into such an existence? There were several reasons. First, most of them were poor. They had spent their life savings for passage to America and arrived with little left. Needing money to survive, they accepted any job they could get. Usually these jobs required no skill and paid the lowest wage. All that was needed to perform the task associated with them was a strong back!

Another reason why immigrants were forced into slums is that, by the turn of the century, there was a surplus of unskilled workers in America. There was so much competition for jobs that immigrants had become expendable. This means they were no longer needed as they had once been. Facing such a situation, they were cheated and taken advantage of by dishonest owners who cared nothing for their welfare.

A final reason for the sad plight of the immigrants was the lack of laws to regulate housing effectively. Owners and landlords could get by with renting rooms and apartments that were dirty and rundown. They could get by with neglecting to make badly needed repairs. They could do these things because public opinion was on their side. Few people cared what happened to immigrants. As was mentioned earlier, many people felt that immigrants were a threat to the American way of life and should be sent back to their native lands.

Matters began to improve after 1890. This was due largely to the efforts of such reformers as Jacob Riis and Jane Addams. Riis was a Danish-American newspaper reporter who wrote about how immigrants lived. His writings awoke many Americans to the conditions of the slums and led to laws that corrected the worst of them.

Jane Addams founded Hull House in Chicago. Hull House was a place where immigrants could go for help of almost any kind. They could get a hot meal, learn to cook, or take classes in English. Similar sites, called settlement houses, sprang up in other cities and did much to make the lives of immigrants easier.

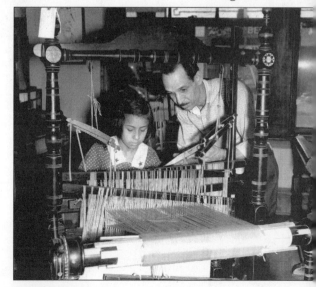

A young girl working at Hull House in the 1930s. Hull House offered a variety of services to immigrants.

Name _____ Date _____

Write a Persuasive Letter to a Friend

In Chapter 3, you imagined yourself an immigrant writing a letter in which you tried to persuade a friend back home to emigrate to America.

Now, imagine you are an immigrant living in a crowded, unheated tenement building in New York City in the year 1900. Write a letter to a friend in your native town or village giving reasons why he or she should not emigrate.

July 8, 1900

Dear _____,

_____

_____

_____

_____

_____

_____

_____

_____

_____

_____

_____

_____

_____

_____

_____

_____

_____

Your friend,

_____

From Everyday Life: Immigration © Good Year Books.

Name _____ Date _____

Fill In a Venn Diagram

In Chapter 4, you completed a Venn diagram comparing Atlantic crossings during the Old Immigration and New Immigration periods. Here is another Venn diagram for you to fill in. This time, indicate how life was different for immigrants during the two periods.

Write significant facts about each period in the appropriate place. List features common to both where the circles overlap.

Old Immigration

Both

New Immigration

Name _____ Date _____

Play the Role of an Editor

Every immigrant community had a newspaper printed in its native language. These newspapers kept immigrants informed about what was happening back home and provided them with valuable information concerning the strange ways of America.

Immigrant newspapers, like newspapers everywhere, featured columnists who offered advice to people with problems. Sometimes, these problems had to do with romance.

Pretend you are an editor of an immigrant newspaper who received this letter.

Dear Editor,

I am a young man, now almost twenty years old. I have met a wonderful girl I wish to marry. But I have a problem. My problem is that the young lady I love is of a different nationality. She speaks little of my language and understands little of my ways. The same holds true for me concerning her.

My parents are against our marrying, which puts me in somewhat of a quandary. I love this girl and, in spite of our differences, I want to marry her. But I also do not wish to hurt my parents who have been so good to me.

What should I do?

On the lines below, write what answer, or advice, you would give to the young man who wrote the letter.

_____

_____

_____

_____

_____

_____

_____

_____

_____

_____

_____

_____

_____

From Everyday Life: Immigration ©Good Year Books.

Name _____ Date _____

Make a Shoe Box Diorama

While most immigrants who came to America in the years following the Civil War never left the large cities of the Northeast, some did make their way to the farmlands of the Great Plains. Many of the settlers who turned the Plains into a productive region were from Finland and the Scandinavian countries. Although they confronted special problems of their own, these immigrants at least escaped the misery of living in crowded tenements and working in unhealthy sweatshops and factories.

Most immigrants who settled on the Great Plains built houses of sod. This was because there are very few trees on the Plains. Can you imagine living in a house made of clumps of grass and dirt? Many people did, and they were quite happy doing so.

Find pictures of sod houses in an encyclopedia or some other resource. Then make a shoe box diorama depicting such a house and its surroundings. You might also include members of a family at work, farm animals, a windmill, or any other scenes and objects associated with a homestead on the Great Plains.

Some Materials That Will Be Helpful:

1. A large shoe box

2. Modeling clay or small figurines of people and animals

3. Construction paper

4. Cardboard

5. Watercolors, crayons, or magic markers

6. Scissors

7. Glue or paste

On the lines below, write a paragraph describing the scene depicted in your diorama.

_____

_____

_____

_____

_____

_____

_____

_____

From Everyday Life: Immigration ©Good Year Books.

Working in Sweatshops and Other Places

Immigrants who came to America during the Old Immigration were fortunate. Jobs were plentiful, and land was still available for farming. Opportunities abounded for those who were willing to work hard.

Even though these earlier immigrants had the option of moving inland to find work, most stayed in the big cities of the northeast. In this respect, they were no different than the immigrants who came during the New Immigration. They took jobs in textile mills and other factories, and some of them, especially the Irish, suffered from the same hatred and discrimination.

But there was one big difference in the two immigration periods. That difference had to do with jobs. Immigrants who came from southern and eastern Europe after 1880 found that jobs had become scarce. America's roads and canals had largely been built. Her railroads crisscrossed the country and her cities were booming. Her farmland had been gobbled up. There was little left for unskilled laborers to do except drift into factories and mines.

Competition for jobs was keen. Because most immigrants who came from southern and eastern Europe were unskilled peasants, they took any job available. Often this meant working in a sweatshop. If you look at the two words that make up *sweatshop,* you can easily see what kind of workplace it was. It usually consisted of one hot, cramped room where people often literally sweated at their labor for more than 12 hours each day. Sometimes they worked as long as 18 hours.

Lewis Hine's 1900 photograph of a family working together in a home sweatshop. Note the cramped conditions of their work area.

Most sweatshops were associated with the garment industry. Because clothing was produced in great quantities, factories could not house all the machines and workers they needed. So factory owners contracted out much of the work to *sweaters.*

A sweater was a middleman who set up a home factory in one room of his tenement apartment. Here as many as twenty workers, bent over sewing machines, put pieces of clothing together. A few workers had the means to buy their own machines. Most, however, had to rent one.

From *Everyday Life: Immigration* © Good Year Books.

Sweatshops were not only hot and cramped, they were usually dirty and unsanitary as well. Sewers who worked from before dawn until after dusk never saw the sun. This was especially hard on little children forced to labor beside their parents. These children worked the same long hours, performing simple tasks such as threading needles and cutting loose threads. They rarely had a chance to play or go to school. Many died of tuberculosis and other job-related diseases within a few years.

With immigrants desperately in need of jobs, sweaters could get by with paying the lowest of wages. A male worker, if he hurried and turned out as many pieces of work as possible, might earn a whopping $5 a week! Usually he earned much less. Women received lower pay simply because they were women. And how about a child who endured the same pitiful working conditions and the same hours? Somewhere between 50¢ and $1.50 a week!

In addition to being hot and unsanitary, sweatshops were dangerous. Sometimes the danger was due to the owners' practice of locking all the doors to the rooms where people worked. They did not want workers "wasting time" going outside to cool off and get a breath of fresh air. It was only natural that such a practice would lead to disaster.

Probably the worst disaster associated with sweatshops occurred in 1911 in New York City. It was such a tragedy that it led to new safety and health laws for public buildings. But the laws came too late to prevent the deaths of 146 workers at the Triangle Shirtwaist Company. Most of these workers were young women.

All that remained of the Triangle Shirtwaist Company in New York after a fire that killed 146 workers.

The Triangle Shirtwaist Company was a sweatshop located on the seventh floor of a building in New York. On March 25, 1911, the sweatshop caught fire. With all exits locked, the women were trapped. Some jumped to their deaths on the streets below. The others died in the flames that quickly engulfed the shop. It was a tragedy that never should have happened.

Not all poor immigrants worked in factory sweatshops. In homes where mothers could not leave young children, families labored together in

From *Everyday Life: Immigration* © Good Year Books.

sweatshops of their own. Boarders who lived with them often joined in the labor. Even the youngest of children were given tasks to do. Sometimes a family made artificial flowers. Sometimes they made cigars or garters. Regardless of the item being produced, children as young as two and three worked alongside their parents. It took many hands to put food on an immigrant family's table.

Conditions in factories and mines were as bad as those in sweatshops. In addition to long hours and low pay, workers toiled in environments that were even more unhealthy and dangerous. Accidents were frequent and deaths on the job commonplace. But greedy owners didn't care. There were always lines of immigrants waiting at the gates of plants and mines to take the places of those who had fallen.

While most immigrants who arrived during the New Immigration stayed in New York and other large northeastern cities, some did find their way inland. Many took jobs in the stockyards and meat-packing plants of the Midwest. Others wandered to the coal fields of western Pennsylvania. But wherever they went, the story was always the same. Hard work, low pay, and unsafe working conditions were the lot of the immigrant worker.

Few places were more dangerous than the slaughterhouses and meat-packing plants of Chicago. The terrible conditions that existed there were exposed by a writer named Upton Sinclair in his book *The Jungle*. Although it is a novel, *The Jungle* accurately describes what it was like to work in a

Men at work in a Chicago slaughterhouse. With few government regulations to guarantee their safety, workers in meat-packing plants were exposed to constant danger.

slaughterhouse or meat-packing plant. To put it simply, conditions could not have been worse. Men and boys had fingers and hands lopped off from sharp knives and stamping machines. Anyone with a minor cut was apt to see it develop into a festering sore that never healed. Many who worked in the slaughterhouses suffered from tuberculosis, and those who worked in the chilling rooms often came down with rheumatism. But there is more! Sometimes men fell into large vats of bubbling lard, the melted-

From *Everyday Life: Immigration* ©Good Year Books.

down fat of pigs and hogs once widely used in cooking. There was little left of these unfortunate workers by the time their bodies were fished out.

Boys who worked in the meat-packing plants suffered too. They were exposed to the same dangers as the men, and often their suffering was much greater. Upton Sinclair tells of one boy who, being very poor, could not afford to take a streetcar to work. He walked every morning, even in the dead of winter. One day in late February, when the temperature hovered around twenty degrees below zero, the boy reported to work screaming in pain. A concerned coworker immediately yanked the boy's shawl from his head and began rubbing his ears. After one or two vigorous rubs, the boy's frozen ears broke completely off!

Finally, there were the young boys apprenticed to the coal mines of Pennsylvania. They worked in a large building called the breakers. Their job was to separate good coal from rocks and slate. For more than 12 hours each day, they leaned over a chute through which coal came to them by way of a conveyor belt. Using only their hands, they had to reach in quickly and remove everything except pure coal before it proceeded to a washer. Because

Two young workers in a textile mill. Note how the boy on the right must stand on some object to reach the spools.

anthracite coal is very hard, boys were lucky if they only received bruised fingers. Sometimes their fingers got caught in the machinery and were cut off. A few boys even fell into the chute and suffocated under the piles of coal. All this for 60¢ a day, six days a week!

The writings of Upton Sinclair and others called attention to the horrible conditions that existed in our nation's factories and mines. As a result, Americans were shocked into action. They demanded that laws be passed to correct such abuses and to regulate child labor as well. In time, their demands were met.

Young boys at work in the breakers of a coal mine. Ill-health, injury, and even death sometimes resulted from the conditions under which they worked.

From *Everyday Life: Immigration* © Good Year Books.

Name _____ Date _____

Solve a Sweatshop Puzzle

Fill in the sentences at the bottom of the page to complete this puzzle about sweatshops. The sentences are based on what you read about sweatshops in the chapter.

```
        S _ _ _ _ _
      _ W _ _ _ _ _
    _ _ _ E _ _ _
      _ A _ _ _ _ _
    _ _ T _ _ _ _ _ _
  _ _ _ _ S _ _
    _ H _ _ _ _ _ _ _
    _ O _ _ _
    _ P _ _ _ _ _ _ _
    S _ _
```

1. People who worked in garment-industry sweatshops often had to rent _____ machines.

2. A _____ was a middleman who ran a sweatshop and supplied materials for the people who worked there.

3. By working as fast as he could, a male worker in a garment sweatshop might earn as much as _____ dollars a week.

4. Most sweatshops were connected with the _____ industry.

5. Some families worked at home making _____ flowers.

6. Tuberculosis and other _____ were characteristic of garment industry sweatshops.

7. A fire at the Triangle _____ Company in 1911 killed 146 workers.

8. Most of the workers killed in the Triangle disaster were young _____.

9. _____ is work paid for by the amount produced.

10. The _____ was something sweatshop workers who toiled from before dawn until after dusk never saw.

From Everyday Life: Immigration ©Good Year Books.

Name _____ Date _____

Draw Conclusions from Your Reading

Read each of the following situations. Then draw your own conclusions to answer the questions. Write your answers on the lines provided.

1. Many immigrant children worked long hours in sweatshops and other places. They had little time for play or other activities. The joy of simply being children was taken away from them at an early age. How do you think their attitudes about life were affected by their existence?

   _____

   _____

2. Other immigrant children were more fortunate. They got to go to school, where they mingled and played with children of different nationalities and religious backgrounds. How would their experiences cause them to grow up differently than their parents?

   _____

   _____

3. Many immigrants grew weary of the day-to-day struggle just to survive. They watched helplessly as their children went hungry and often died long before their time. Others never found a job—even a job of the lowest kind. In desperation, some turned to a life of crime. What can you conclude from this behavior?

   _____

   _____

4. Many years went by before laws were passed that ended child labor and improved the lot of workers in factories and other places. What does this tell you about American public opinion regarding child laborers some 100 years ago?

   _____

   _____

From Everyday Life: Immigration ©Good Year Books.

Name _____ Date _____

Name Those Synonyms

Here is a list of 20 words taken from Chapter 9. Write two synonyms for each on the lines provided. The way each word is used in the text is indicated by its part of speech in parentheses.

1. fortunate (adj) _____ _____

2. option (n) _____ _____

3. hatred (n) _____ _____

4. practice (n) _____ _____

5. rarely (adv) _____ _____

6. keen (adj) _____ _____

7. artificial (adj) _____ _____

8. wandered (v) _____ _____

9. accurately (adv) _____ _____

10. labor (v) _____ _____

11. exposed (v) _____ _____

12. prevent (v) _____ _____

13. task (n) _____ _____

14. unsanitary (adj) _____ _____

15. regulate (v) _____ _____

16. endured (v) _____ _____

17. minor (adj) _____ _____

18. shocked (v) _____ _____

19. horrible (adj) _____ _____

20. plentiful (adj) _____ _____

From Everyday Life: Immigration ©Good Year Books.

Name _____ Date _____

Recall Information You Have Read

How well do you remember what you have read? Recalling information is an important skill that every student should strive to master.

At right are questions having to do with Chapter 9. See how many you can answer without referring back to the text.

1. What prevented immigrants who came during the New Immigration from finding work building canals and laying railroad track, as earlier immigrants had done?

   _____

2. Why were sweatshops so named?

   _____

3. With what industry were most sweatshops associated?

   _____

4. Who was a sweater?

   _____

5. How much did children who worked in sweatshops earn?

   _____

6. What happened at the Triangle Shirtwaist Company in 1911?

   _____

7. What kind of products did families make in home workshops?

   _____

8. What did author Upton Sinclair describe in his book *The Jungle?*

   _____

9. What was the job of the young boys who worked in the breakers?

   _____

CHAPTER 10

Making Contributions

In spite of the difficulties they faced, immigrants have made—and are continuing to make—lasting contributions to their adopted country. They have enriched and strengthened American society and culture many times over, and for this we should be grateful.

Take any aspect of American life. Whether you are thinking of food, language, holidays, clothing, or anything else, immigrants have had a tremendous impact. Let's consider what is surely one of your favorite areas: food. Do you like ravioli, spaghetti, and pizza? Thank those immigrants who came from Italy. What about shish kebab, which is lamb cut into cubes and broiled on a skewer? That is an Armenian dish. (Armenia is part of what is now Turkey.) Then there are other favorites, such as Chinese egg rolls and Mexican tacos and enchiladas. But none can probably compare to the classic "American" hamburger, which supposedly originated in the German city of Hamburg and was brought to this country by German immigrants.

Want more? Try Japanese sukiyaki or Russian beef Stroganoff. All right, so you're a vegetarian. You might like minestrone, an Italian soup, or borscht, a Russian beet soup served with sour cream. You might also enjoy Greek stuffed salad or Thai tofu curry. The list is endless. It covers everything from soups and starters to full-course meals. You can thank those immigrants from all parts of the world who brought these and other delicious foods with them when they emigrated to America.

A street in the Chinese section of an American city. Large cities came to have their "Chinatowns," "Little Italys," "Little Polands," and other districts as a result of large-scale immigration in the 19th and early-20th centuries.

And what about language? Most of us may speak English, but it is an English punctuated with words borrowed from other languages. We go to *kindergarten* (German), enjoy *fiestas* (Spanish), and, if we're rich, have *chauffeurs* (French) who drive us around. Some Southerners stay busy keeping pesky *armadillos* (Spanish) from uprooting their grass in their search for earthworms and other delicacies.

Immigrants have also contributed to the customs and traditions surrounding many of our holidays. Nowhere is this more apparent than in the

From *Everyday Life: Immigration* ©Good Year Books.

Christian celebration of Christmas. German immigrants brought over the idea of Christmas trees, as well as the custom of decorating them with ornaments and lights (candles). And Santa Claus? That name derived from the difficulty American children had in pronouncing *Sinter Klaas*, which is what the little Dutch children of New York in the 1600s called Saint Nicholas. To the children of the English colonies, Santa Claus was close enough!

Every nationality or religious group today can thank immigrants for bringing their beliefs and traditions with them to America. Chinese Americans celebrate the Chinese New Year, while immigrants from Vietnam have transported their celebration of *Tet*, the lunar new year observed in Southeast Asia. And think of people of the Jewish faith. Many years ago, Jewish immigrants brought with them all the customs and ceremonies associated with their religion.

A family decorates a Christmas tree in this engraving from the 19th century. The custom of the Christmas tree was brought to America by German immigrants.

Immigrants also gave us a number of tangible things. The log cabin was a contribution of the Swedes who settled in what became Delaware and New Jersey. Can you imagine the early American frontier without log cabins? What would settlers have lived in—trees?

Does your school have a chorus? That is a contribution of German immigrants. Does your town or city have a symphony orchestra? That is also a German contribution. Do you enjoy bowling and ice skating? These pastimes were introduced to America by the Dutch.

Countless individual immigrants have left their marks on America. Some arrived with money and succeeded right from the start. Others managed to rise above their humble beginnings to make notable contributions in business, education, science, and other fields. A few of these are mentioned in the paragraphs that follow.

One immigrant from Scotland to whom we owe much is Alexander Graham Bell. I'm sure you know that he invented the telephone. Can you imagine life today without this indispensable (essential) device? Bell, who had previously been a teacher of the hearing impaired, stumbled upon the

From Everyday Life: Immigration © Good Year Books.

invention of the telephone in 1876 while trying to devise a better hearing aid for one of his former students, Mabel Hubbard. He married Miss Hubbard one year after developing his amazing invention.

Almost as integral to daily modern life as the telephone is television. Could we survive without it? We could, but for some of us it might be a frightening experience! We can thank Vladimir Zworykin, a Russian immigrant, for developing the television camera and the television picture tube. He produced both in 1923. Although considered something of a novelty at first, by the late 1950s television had become a permanent fixture in most American homes.

You are no doubt familiar with Albert Einstein. Einstein was a brilliant German physicist who had to flee Nazi Germany in 1933 because of his Jewish faith. He came to the United States and accepted a position as a professor at the Institute for Advanced Study in Princeton, New Jersey. It was Einstein who contacted President Franklin Roosevelt in 1939 about the possibility of making an atomic bomb. Einstein hated violence and the thought of such a weapon, but he believed the United States should develop it before Nazi Germany succeeded in doing so.

An undated photograph of Elizabeth Blackwell, the first woman to receive a medical degree in America. Her success opened doors for other women.

Mention was made of Jacob Riis in Chapter 8. Riis emigrated from Denmark in 1870 and became a journalist and reformer in the United States. The stories he wrote for various New York newspapers helped end some of the worst abuses in that city's slums. He also led the fight for the construction of city parks and playgrounds.

Immigrant women have also made important contributions. Elizabeth Blackwell was born in England and emigrated to the United States in 1831 at the age of ten. She made history in 1849 by receiving the first medical degree ever awarded to a woman. Her courage and determination opened the door for other women to enter the medical profession.

You may be too young to have heard of Greta Garbo, but older Americans remember her well. She was a Swedish movie star who came to the United

From *Everyday Life: Immigration* ©Good Year Books.

States in 1926. She was one of Hollywood's leading performers until she suddenly retired in 1941.

Knute Rockne, who came from Norway in 1893, became a great football player and coach at Notre Dame. Irving Berlin emigrated from Russia in 1892 and grew up to become one of America's greatest songwriters. Andrew Carnegie was a Scottish immigrant who made a fortune in the steel business and donated millions of dollars to charity.

The list goes on. Igor Sikorsky came from Russia in 1919 and contributed the first practical single-rotor helicopter in 1939. Arturo Toscanini emigrated from Italy and became one of the world's greatest conductors (orchestra leaders). Carl Schurz was a German immigrant who fought in the Civil War as a Union general and later became a statesman. John Muir emigrated from Scotland and gained prominence as a naturalist. So did John James Audubon, the son of a French sea captain who came from Haiti and became a famous painter of birds. These and many others contributed their talents and skills to the American way of life.

Perhaps the most noteworthy immigrants, however, are those whose names have not gone down in history. They are the "little people"—those hearty newcomers who brought nothing more to America than their strong backs and their determination to make a better life for themselves.

Those who came during the Old Immigration built roads and canals. They cleared forests and laid miles of railroad track. Many ventured onto the Great Plains and helped turn an arid region into fertile farmland.

Those who came during the New Immigration also achieved success, although in an indirect way. While most of them arrived poor and remained that way, they watched with pride as their children and grandchildren became "Americanized" and made contributions to their adopted land. It was these younger immigrants who became the doctors, lawyers, and educators that helped guide our nation through the first half of the twentieth century.

Swedish movie star Greta Garbo during the filming of a scene from a 1926 movie. Garbo came to Hollywood from Sweden at the age of 19.

Knute Rockne, famous Notre Dame football coach, diagramming a play for an assistant. In 13 seasons, Rockne guided Notre Dame to over 100 victories.

From Everyday Life: Immigration ©Good Year Books.

Name _____ Date _____

Name That Famous Immigrant

In the word box are the names of 12 immigrants who became quite famous after coming to the United States. Choose from the names to fill in the blank line in front of each statement.

John James Audubon	Greta Garbo
Alexander Graham Bell	Jacob Riis
Irving Berlin	Knute Rockne
Elizabeth Blackwell	Carl Schurz
Andrew Carnegie	Igor Sikorsky
Albert Einstein	Vladimir Zworykin

1. _____ "I was the first woman doctor in the United States."

2. _____ "My newspaper stories helped correct abuses in New York City's slums."

3. _____ "I developed America's first practical helicopter."

4. _____ "I studied and painted birds."

5. _____ "I was a famous football coach at Notre Dame."

6. _____ "I was a Swedish-born movie star."

7. _____ "I made a fortune in the steel business."

8. _____ "I suggested the making of an atomic bomb to President Roosevelt."

9. _____ "I invented the telephone."

10. _____ "You can thank me for television."

11. _____ "I came from Germany and became a Union general in the Civil War."

12. _____ "I became a famous songwriter."

From Everyday Life: Immigration ©Good Year Books.

Name _____ Date _____

Make a Mobile About Famous Immigrants

Make a mobile depicting famous immigrants and their contributions to America. You can choose from among those mentioned in the chapter or select others with whom you may be familiar. Or perhaps you might want your mobile to be a combination of both.

Here Is What You Will Need:

1. A large clothes hanger

2. Different-colored construction paper

3. String

4. Hole punch

5. Felt-tip pen

6. Pieces of stiff wire

Here Is What You Do:

1. Cut different colors of construction paper into tags measuring about 2" x 3" in size. Cut tags into various shapes: squares, circles, triangles, rectangles, stars, and so on.

2. On one side of each tag, write the name of a famous immigrant. On the other side, write the contribution he or she made.

3. Punch a hole at the top of each tag.

4. Insert and tie a piece of string through the hole at the top of each tag. Make your pieces of string different lengths so you can stagger the tags on the clothes hanger.

5. Attach the tags to the bottom of the clothes hanger.

6. Make a sign reading "Famous Immigrants" and attach it to the top of the hanger.

To make a more detailed mobile, cut pieces of stiff wire in lengths of about 6". Slightly bend each piece in the middle to give it a rainbow shape. Attach a tag to each end of the wire strips. Tie different lengths of string to the middle of the various pieces of wire and hang them from the bottom of the clothes hanger.

Name _____ Date _____

Write a Lead Paragraph for *The Boston Blab*

Imagine yourself a reporter for *The Boston Blab* on the day Alexander Graham Bell sent his first message on the telephone. Write the lead paragraph of a story that would go along with the headlines. Be sure to include answers to the five *W* questions (*Who? What? When? Where?* and *Why?*) that all lead paragraphs should contain.

Before writing your paragraph, you might want to read about Alexander Graham Bell in an encyclopedia.

The Boston Blab

★★★★★★★★★★★★★★★★★★★★★★

**** March 10, 1876 ****

YOUNG SCOTSMAN MAKES HISTORY

A.G. Bell Sends First Telephone Message

_____
_____
_____
_____
_____
_____
_____
_____
_____
_____
_____
_____
_____
_____
_____
_____

From *Everyday Life: Immigration* © Good Year Books.

Name _____ Date _____

Distinguish Between Fact and Opinion

Below is a conversation that might have taken place between two students after their class had just completed a discussion of immigration and the contributions immigrants have made to American society. Carefully read the dialogue, and mark each statement **F** if you think it is a fact or **O** if you consider it only an opinion. Remember that a fact is a statement that can be proven, while an opinion is simply a strong belief.

_____ **Student #1:** "Immigrants certainly have made many contributions to America."

_____ **Student #2:** "Yes, every single immigrant who came contributed in some way to America becoming a better place."

_____ **Student #1:** "That was especially true of those who came during the Old Immigration. They were so much smarter than those who arrived later."

_____ **Student #2:** "Well, I don't agree with that, but those who came earlier did have a greater opportunity to succeed. There were more jobs and land available then."

_____ **Student #1:** "Speaking of opportunity and success, it is easy to see that Vladimir Zworykin made the greatest contribution of any immigrant."

_____ **Student #2:** "Yes, I agree. Television is the most important invention ever made."

_____ **Student #1:** "What do you think about the telephone? It certainly has had an impact on America."

_____ **Student #2:** "True, but immigrants have contributed more than just inventions. Take Irving Berlin. He became a famous songwriter."

_____ **Student #1:** "And Elizabeth Blackwell. She was America's first woman doctor."

_____ **Student #2:** "And Greta Garbo. She was the greatest actress Hollywood has ever seen."

_____ **Student #1:** "And don't forget Knute Rockne at Notre Dame. Now, there was a football coach. Modern-day coaches are wimps compared to him."

_____ **Student #2:** "Well, that may be true. I wouldn't know. I don't like football. It's the dumbest game anyone ever thought of."

From Everyday Life: Immigration © Good Year Books.

CHAPTER II

Continuing to Come

On January 1, 1892, fifteen-year-old Annie Moore from Ireland became the first immigrant to pass through the gates of Ellis Island. She had no way of knowing that over the next 60 years, more than 12 million others would follow her. She also had no way of knowing that one day America would severely restrict immigration and even close Ellis Island as a receiving station.

You learned in Chapter 7 that government restrictions on immigration began in the late 1800s. By 1929 the total number of immigrants allowed to enter each year was reduced to 150,000. Quotas were based on the percentage of each nationality in the total U.S. population of 1890. Since the vast majority of immigrants up to that time had come from northern and western Europe, it is easy to see that quotas were slanted in their favor. Of the 150,000 allowed to immigrate, only 16 percent could come from southern and eastern Europe. Asia and other parts of the world received an allotment of 2 percent. This meant that 82 percent of the immigrants who came after 1929 were from northern and western Europe.

Nearly 10,000 immigrants, mostly Hispanics, celebrate their naturalization in Miami's Orange Bowl in 1984. The ceremony was the largest naturalization event in American history.

In reality, not many people came at all in the decade following 1929. Strict immigration laws and the beginning of the Great Depression reduced immigration to a trickle. More people actually left the United States during the Depression than entered it. Conditions were no better in America at that time than they were elsewhere.

Attitudes toward immigration changed somewhat after World War II. In 1948, some 400,000 refugees from war-torn Europe were allowed to come to the United States. In 1953, another act of Congress permitted 200,000 more to enter from the Communist nations of eastern Europe. Three years later, an unsuccessful revolution in Hungary brought an additional 20,000. Finally, thousands of Cubans fleeing the Communist takeover of their country in 1959 were allowed to enter after 1961.

Although political refugees from other nations were welcomed, general immigration laws were still based on the old national-origins quota system. President Harry S. Truman vigorously opposed such restrictions, saying that

From Everyday Life: Immigration ©Good Year Books.

they violated the principles upon which America was founded. Presidents Eisenhower, Kennedy, and Johnson who followed agreed. Each of these presidents was in favor of doing away with the national-origins system. Each felt that immigrants from every region of the world should have an equal chance to come to the United States.

In 1965, a new immigration law did away with the old quota system and gave immigrants from Asia, Africa, and southern Europe equal access to America. Although the total number of immigrants allowed was still limited, the law at least did not favor one group over another.

Later immigration laws caused a total shift in immigration patterns. In recent years the vast majority of immigrants have come from Asia and Latin America. War and unrest in southeast Asia have brought thousands of Vietnamese and others seeking refuge. Extreme poverty in Latin America has caused thousands more to look to the United States for relief. Perhaps 75 percent of all immigrants today come from these two regions.

Where have recent arrivals settled? In general, they have concentrated in six states. These six states are California, New York, Florida, Texas, New Jersey, and Illinois. Have they been welcomed? Opinion is divided.

This wall, built at Tijuana, Mexico, in 1984, was an attempt to stop illegal Mexican immigration at the California border.

Those who support immigration think America should forever remain a haven for the oppressed and poor of the world. They further contend that immigrants contribute much to the economy. On the one hand, they point out, America benefits from scientists and engineers who flee or willingly leave other countries. On the other, they argue that unskilled immigrants take jobs most Americans do not want, such as migrant farm work.

Americans who oppose immigration are just as outspoken. They stress that language differences prevent immigrants from blending into the mainstream of American life. They also worry that immigrants take jobs away from other workers and pose serious social and health problems. Finally, they point out that the influx of immigrants to certain sections of the country (Florida, for example) places a strain on educational and welfare systems.

Of special concern are illegal immigrants. Most of these come from Mexico and cross over into the United

From Everyday Life: Immigration © Good Year Books.

States along Texas's long border with that nation. Others cross the border into Arizona and California. Efforts to keep them out have proven unsuccessful. Laws punishing employers who hire illegal immigrants have reduced the flow somewhat, but the tide of people still comes. Many Mexicans and others are willing to take any chance and risk any danger to enter the United States.

And the risks are considerable. Immigrants from Mexico and other Latin American countries have been cheated, robbed, raped, beaten, and murdered. Horror stories can be told of those who paid money to be smuggled into the United States, only to end up abandoned in the desert or elsewhere. Sometimes they are abandoned on foot, but there is at least one recorded incident of a group being left to die in a locked truck!

In July 1980, a small group of illegal immigrants from El Salvador paid a coyote (a smuggler of immigrants) $50 apiece to be driven to the Arizona border. There they were met by another coyote in an old moving van, to whom they also paid $50. The second smuggler informed the Salvadorans that they would be taken to good-paying jobs in a large city. Instead, the van drove around the desert in circles for several hours, going nowhere. Sometime during the night, the driver stopped, locked the occupants in, and walked away. Twelve people died inside the locked truck before it was discovered the next day.

Cuban refugees attempting to reach the United States in a home-made raft. They are holding empty containers as they beg for water.

Other stories exist of illegal immigrants becoming virtual slaves to people they trusted to help them. Some have been forced to work in modern-day versions of sweatshops. Others, particularly children, have been made to stand on street corners for long hours selling trinkets or similar items. Worse has happened to many others.

In spite of the risks involved and the resentment they often face, the immigrants continue to come. During 1996 alone, more than two million newcomers either entered the country illegally or stayed on after their work visas expired. Add to this the more than 900,000 who entered legally, and it is easy to see that America is still thought of as the land of opportunity by the unfortunate peoples of the world.

From *Everyday Life: Immigration* © Good Year Books.

Today, roughly 10 percent of Americans are foreign born. About one-fourth of these are from Mexico. Others have come in large numbers from the Philippines, Taiwan, Cuba, El Salvador, and the Dominican Republic. Still others were born in Canada, Great Britain, Germany, and Poland. A sprinkling of immigrants have come from just about every other nation of the world.

You will remember from Chapter 6 that Ellis Island was closed as a receiving station in 1954. Today, immigrants entering the United States legally usually arrive by plane. They apply for visas at U.S. consulates in their respective countries, and, if they have no infectious disease or criminal record, they are on their way.

To gain a better understanding of the immigrant experience and its impact on America, one should visit the Ellis Island Immigration Museum in New York. The museum occupies the buildings that once served as the main U.S. immigrant receiving station. Almost $160 million was collected from private sources to restore the aged center. Today, it stands as a monument to all those immigrants who came to America between 1892 and 1954.

Visitors to the museum find it difficult not to feel the anxiety and the emotions experienced by the immigrants of years ago. The Great Hall of the main room and the various other rooms that make up the museum are filled with reminders. There are suitcases, baskets, and other items that once belonged to immigrants. But mostly there are pictures—hundreds of them. These pictures show immigrants going through the various stages of processing, which included the intelligence tests and the physical exams they had heard of and feared. A close look reveals the anxiety and uncertainly on their faces.

But there is another look that is apparent on the faces of many. That is the look of determination and hope. For it was determination and hope that brought millions of immigrants to America many years ago, and it is determination and hope that continues to bring them today.

Hispanic immigrants pledge their loyalty to the United States in the citizenship ceremony held in the Orange Bowl in 1984.

From *Everyday Life: Immigration* © Good Year Books.

Name _____ Date _____

Solve More Immigration Word Problems

Here are four word problems having to do with immigration today. Work each in the space provided, and write its answer on the line given.

1. The Immigration and Naturalization Service reported that approximately 720,000 legal immigrants entered the United States in 1995. One year later, this number had increased by 27 percent. How many legal immigrants were admitted in 1996? _____ immigrants

2. Of the total number of legal immigrants admitted in 1996, approximately 163,000 came from Mexico. What percent of the total number did Mexicans represent?
_____%

3. California, with 201,529 immigrants, led the way as the place of settlement for those who came legally in 1996. New York was next with 154,095, followed by Texas with 83,385 and Florida with 79,461. How many legal immigrants settled in these four states altogether? _____ immigrants

4. About 2,700,000 Mexicans entered the United States illegally in 1996. By contrast, there were 335,000 illegal immigrants from El Salvador. How many more illegal immigrants came from Mexico? _____ immigrants

From *Everyday Life: Immigration* ©Good Year Books.

Name _____ Date _____

Create a Dialogue

Juan is an unemployed Mexican laborer with a problem. If he does not find work soon, he, his wife, Conchita, and their three small children will go hungry. Hopes for finding employment in his village are slim.

In desperation, Juan has almost decided to risk crossing the border into the United States to look for work. Conchita is against such a move, pointing out the many dangers involved.

Create a dialogue in which Juan and Conchita discuss what should be done.

Name _____ Date _____

Solve an Immigration Crossword

Across

2. What Ellis Island is today

4. State receiving the most immigrants

6. The _____ Depression

9. Most illegal immigrants come from this country

12. Ellis _____

13. State receiving the second largest number of immigrants

Down

1. Country taken over by Communists in 1959

3. President _____ Truman

4. A smuggler of immigrants

5. The Dominican _____

7. Percentage of foreign-born Americans today

8. Many immigrants come from this continent

10. The national-_____ quota system

11. _____ Salvador

From *Everyday Life: Immigration* © Good Year Books.

Answers to Activities

Chapter 1
Distinguish Between Fact and Opinion
1. F 2. F 3. O 4. F 5. O 6. O
7. O 8. F 9. O 10. F 11. F 12. O
13. F

Find the Main Idea
Answers should be similar to the following:

Paragraph 1—People from many religious groups and walks of life came to America.

Paragraph 6—The Pilgrims were concerned that their children would grow up more Dutch than English.

Paragraph 7—Crossing the Atlantic was a dangerous and difficult journey.

Paragraph 10—The Puritans were intolerant of people with opposing religious views.

Paragraph 14—The Quakers welcomed all settlers to Pennsylvania.

Paragraph 17—Some colonists who came to America were criminals or had served time in jail for minor offenses.

Chapter 2
Draw Conclusions from Your Reading
Answers should be similar to the following:
1. Conditions in the South favored large farms and plantations, resulting in slavery's becoming firmly established. Because the climate and geography of New England kept farms small, slavery never became a permanent factor.
2. The Indians of the Americas were more susceptible to disease and the hardships of forced labor than were slaves brought from Africa. In addition, it was difficult for African slaves to run away inasmuch as they had no place to hide.
3. They preferred death to being sent to the New World as slaves.

Interpret a Population Line Graph
1. 800% 2. 3,700,000 3. 3 4. 700,000
5. 400,000

Recall Information from the Narrative
1. Portugal
2. African slaves in Portugal and Spain were often granted their freedom, after which they could do as they pleased.
3. West
4. Because they were packed so tightly into the holds of slave ships.
5. Virginia
6. An eleven-year-old African boy who was captured and sold to slave traders
7. Fifty-three slaves mutinied, took over the ship, and sailed it north off the coast of the United States. They were captured off Long Island and brought to trial. Surprisingly, they were freed and allowed to return to Africa.
8. They led slave rebellions.
9. Black Codes were laws that were designed to keep slaves under strict control.

Chapter 3
Brush Up on Your European Geography
1. England (London); Northern Ireland (Belfast); Scotland (Edinburgh); Wales (Cardiff) 2. Dublin 3. Norway (Oslo); Sweden (Stockholm); Denmark (Copenhagen) 4. Helsinki 5. 1871
6. Alps

Distinguish Between Sentences and Fragments
1. F 2. S 3. F 4. F 5. S 6. F
7. S 8. S 9. F
Students' sentences will vary.

Chapter 4
Fill in a Venn Diagram
Responses will vary but might include the following:

Old Immigration—Ship sinkings were common; A voyage took about 40 days; Immigrants died of various diseases; Food was poor.

Both—Conditions in steerage were crowded; Seasickness was a problem; Washing facilities were limited.

New Immigration—Immigrants were treated better; A voyage took only 10 days; There were more nationalities and languages to contend with.

Solve an Immigration Puzzle

1. Liberty   2. Measles   3. Steamships
4. wide   5. steerage   6. forty
7. Dancing   8. twelve   9. wind
10. northern   11. ten

Research and Answer Questions About Typhus

1. Typhus is an infectious disease caused by a rickettsia, a bacteria-like germ carried by fleas, lice, ticks, or mites.
2. High fever; weakness; dark-red spots on the skin; pains in the head, back, and limbs; stupor or delirium
3. Typhus epidemics have occurred during wars and in slums and other areas characterized by unsanitary conditions.
4. Good sanitation and hygiene prevent outbreaks of typhus.
5. With antibiotic drugs
6. People were once sprayed with DDT (now banned because of its effects on the environment) and other insecticides.

Chapter 5

Find the Mean, Mode, and Range

1. 29 million   2. Because no number falls in the middle.   3. 4 million and 6 million   4. 5.8 million   5. 5 million

Use Context Clues to Complete Sentences

population; born; immigrant; flow; turn; eastern; center; receiving; landed; located; obtain; currency; replaced; additional; native; next

Chapter 6

Solve an Ellis Island Crossword

Across: 3. five   4. sixteen   6. Great Hall
11. trachoma   12. thirty
Down: 1. Fiorello   2. mental   3. four
5. banana   6. Garden   7. heart
8. Liberty   9. New York   10. scalp

Solve These Ellis Island Word

Problems

1. 100   2. 83   3. 1,500   4. 258,065

Chapter 7

Make False Statements True

1. German   2. Pennsylvania   3. Irish
4. Order of the Star-Spangled Banner
5. Civil War   6. 1915   7. Catholics
8. potato-crop failure   9. circle
10. Ghettos   11. Chinese
12. northern and western
13. transcontinental railroad

Solve Some Immigration Word Problems

1a. 127,500   1b. 22,500   2. 22
3. 650,000

Chapter 8

Fill in a Venn Diagram

Answers will vary but might include the following:

Old Immigration—There were more jobs; More land was available; Most immigrants were from northern and western Europe; Most, except for the Irish, were Protestants.

Both—Both groups were taken advantage of; Many other Americans resented the presence of immigrants; Both groups saw America as a land of hope; Both tended to congregate in large cities of the northeast.

New Immigration—Newcomers faced more hostility; They were subjected to quotas; They were less skilled; They took any job offered them; Many worked in sweatshops.

Chapter 9

Solve a Sweatshop Puzzle
1. sewing 2. sweater 3. five
4. garment 5. artificial 6. diseases
7. Shirtwaist 8. women 9. Piecework
10. sun

Draw Conclusions from Your Reading
Answers will vary but should be similar to
the following:
1. Children might grow up hardened to life
   and find little to live for.
2. They grew up more tolerant of other
   nationalities and religions and tended to
   think of themselves more as Americans
   than as Russians, Greeks, or other
   peoples.
3. That poverty and hunger often breed
   crime.
4. Americans tended to view children
   simply as smaller adults and failed to
   acknowledge how labor was affecting
   them. As for working conditions, many
   Americans who were well-off cared little
   about the plight of the poor.

Name Those Synonyms
Students' responses will vary, as they can
choose from a number of synonyms for
each word.

Recall Information You Have Read
1. Most canals and railroad tracks had been
   completed by then.
2. Sweatshops were so named because
   workers labored for long hours under
   hot, cramped conditions.
3. The garment industry
4. A sweater was the middleman who
   supplied sweatshop workers with
   materials.
5. Between 50¢ and $1.50 a week
6. A fire caused the deaths of 146 workers,
   most of them young women.
7. Items such as cigars, artificial flowers, and
   garters.
8. The shocking conditions that existed in
   the meat-packing industry.
9. To pick slate and other rocks from good
   coal as it moved along a chute

Chapter 10

Name That Famous Immigrant
1. Elizabeth Blackwell 2. Jacob Riis
3. Igor Sikorsky 4. John James
Audubon 5. Knute Rockne 6. Greta
Garbo 7. Andrew Carnegie 8. Albert
Einstein 9. Alexander Graham Bell
10. Vladimir Zworykin 11. Carl Schurz
12. Irving Berlin

Distinguish Between Fact and Opinion
F, O, O, F, O, O, F, F, F, O,
O, O

Chapter 11

Solve More Immigration Word Problems
1. 914,400 2. 18 3. 518,470
4. 2,365,000

Solve an Immigration Crossword
Across: 2. museum 4. California
    6. Great 9. Mexico 12. Island
    13. New York
Down: 1. Cuba 3. Harry 4. coyote
    5. Republic 7. ten 8. Asia
    10. origins 11. El

Additional Resources

Books for Children

Coleman, Terry. *Going to America*. New York: Pantheon Books, 1972.

The Immigrant's Experience: Cultural Variety and the Melting Pot. An American Education Publications Unit Book. Prepared by Donald W. Oliver and Fred M. Newman. Middletown, Connecticut: American Education Publications, 1970.

Levine, Ellen. *If Your Name Was Changed at Ellis Island*. New York: Scholastic, 1993.

Levinson, Nancy Smiler. *Turn of the Century: Our Nation One Hundred Years Ago*. New York: Lodestar Books, 1994.

Stein, R. Conrad. *Ellis Island*. Chicago: Childrens Press, 1992.

Books for Adults

Blumenthal, Shirley. *Coming to America: Immigrants from Eastern Europe*. New York: Delacorte Press, 1981.

Commons, John R. *Races and Immigrants in America*. New York: Augustus M. Kelley, Publishers, 1967.

May, Ernest R., and the editors of *Life*. "The Progressive Era." Volume 9, 1901–1917, *The Life History of the United States*. New York: Time Incorporated, 1964.

Weisberger, Bernard A., and the editors of *Life*. "Reaching for Empire." Volume 8, *1890–1901, The Life History of the United States*. New York: Time Incorporated, 1964.